Also by Don Gabor

Books
Big Things Happen When You Do the Little Things Right
How to Talk to the People You Love
Speaking Your Mind in 101 Difficult Situations
Talking With Confidence for the Painfully Shy

Audiobooks
How to Start a Conversation
Talking With Confidence for the Painfully Shy
How to Meet People and Make Friends at Work

How to Start a
Conversation
and Make
Friends

Don Gabor

illustrated by Mary Power

A FIRESIDE BOOK
Published by Simon & Schuster
New York   London   Toronto   Sydney   Singapore

FIRESIDE
Rockefeller Center
1230 Avenue of the Americas
New York, NY 10020

Designed by Stratford Publishing Services, Inc.

Manufactured in the United States of America

10   9   8

Library of Congress Cataloging-in-Publication Data
Gabor, Don.
    How to start a conversation and make friends.
    "A Fireside book."
    1. Conversation.   2. Friendship.   I. Title.
BJ2121.G3   1983   248.2'4   83-12038
ISBN 0-684-86801-6

In memory of my sister Ellen,
who never met a stranger.

Acknowledgments

Special thanks go to:

Jeffrey Hollender for the opportunity to develop my conversation course and this book.

My wife, Eileen Cowell, for her loving support, many useful ideas, and sharp editorial eye.

My editors, Cherise Grant and Betsy Radin Herman, for their suggestions and feedback.

My agent, Sheree Bykofsky, for believing in this book project.

My assistant, Patrick Campbell, for helping me complete this revision.

Contents

A Note from the Author

How to Start a Conversation and Make Friends was first published in 1983. Since then, I have written several books and audiotapes, and presented many workshops on conversation skills. Still, even after all my years of teaching and writing about this subject, I realize how much more I have to learn about the art of conversation.

The revisions in this book are based on feedback and questions from hundreds of readers and students, plus additional research and personal experience. I have reorganized the book into four main sections: Starting Conversations, Continuing Conversations, Ending Conversations, and Boosting Your Conversations.

Included in these sections are new and revised chapters on remembering names, conversation styles, talking to people from other countries, mobile phone etiquette, and on-line conversations. I have also highlighted frequently asked questions (FAQs) throughout the text.

Most people want and need human contact, and that connection often takes the form of a simple conversation. The secret to starting conversations and making friends rests on four key principles: 1) Take the initiative and reach out to others; 2) Show genuine interest in people; 3) Treat others with respect and kindness; and 4) Value others and yourself as unique individuals who have much to share and offer one another. When you apply these ideas and the many other skills and tips in this book, you can become a great conversationalist. I hope that this newly revised edition will help you achieve this goal.

Introduction: Meeting New People and Making New Friends

> Good conversation is what makes us interesting. After all, we spend a great deal of our time talking and a great deal of our time listening. Why be bored, why be boring—when you don't have to be either?
> —Edwin Newman (1919–), news commentator

The next time you walk into a room full of people, just listen to them talking! They're all communicating through conversation. Conversation is our main way of expressing our ideas, opinions, goals, and feelings to those we come into contact with. It is also the primary means of beginning and establishing friendships and relationships.

When the "channel of conversation" is open, we can connect and communicate with people around us. If the conversational channel is closed, then starting and sustaining a conversation can be a real problem. This book is based on my "How to Start a Conversation and Make Friends" workshop, and it will show you how to "turn on" your conversational channel and "tune in" to people you meet.

The conversational techniques in this book have been successfully tested in my workshops and proven as methods of starting and sustaining conversations in nearly every situation—including social and business settings. The techniques are presented in an easy-to-master format so you can start improving your communication skills and self-confidence quickly. The techniques are demonstrated in real-life situations so you can practice and learn them within the context of your own lifestyle and at your own pace.

This book can be helpful to a wide variety of people, including:

business executives	parents
consultants	professionals
couples	sales representatives
freelance artists	singles
immigrants	students
managers	teachers
	and many others

If you want more rewarding conversations in professional, social, or personal situations, then this book is for you.

How This Book Can Help You

Many people who attend my workshops are making career changes, and they want to learn how to move easily into a new social and work environment. Salespeople want to know how to converse with clients in an informal (soft-sell) manner, while women executives want to feel confident communicating with their male associates on an equal and nonsexual basis. New residents of the United States want to learn conversational English. Business executives want to learn how not to talk shop while entertaining, and parents want to learn to communicate well with their children and other family members. The list seems endless.

Even good conversationalists sometimes find themselves in situations where the conversation is just not going the way they want it to. This book provides techniques to help you better direct and control the conversation at such times.

Learn to Enjoy Parties While Winning New Friends

Perhaps the most common situation that causes problems for many is meeting new people and socializing at parties and social events. Surveys show that many people feel uncomfortable in a room full of strangers and are anxious about approaching others. This book presents practical skills for meeting new people, making new friends, and developing lasting and meaningful relationships.

Most people want to share their experiences with others. We are constantly searching for others we can relate to on an intellectual, physical, and emotional level. This search can be frustrating and unfulfilling if you aren't able to reach out and communicate. Once you master the basic fundamentals of good conversation and are willing to reach out, you'll be open and available for new friendships and relationships.

You Can Learn to Communicate and Use New Skills

The ability to communicate in an informal and friendly manner is essential for every aspect of a person's business, social, and personal life. Most people can converse with others when they feel confident and comfortable. The problem arises when comfort and confidence are replaced by anxiety and fear. This book will help you identify which communication skills you already have working for you and in which situations you already feel confident.

Once you understand the skills that promote natural conversations, then begin using them in situations where you feel comfortable and confident. You will be able to see how effective you are, while simultaneously integrating these new techniques into your lifestyle.

As you become more confident with your conversational skills in "safe" situations, take some extra risks, and begin to use your new communication skills in situations where you were previously uncomfortable and anxious. You'll be pleasantly surprised to find that your skills will transfer from one situation to another far more easily than you ever imagined. As your control increases, so will your confidence. Your ability to maintain casual and sustained conversations will become part of your personality. Don't think about the skills and techniques too much; just let them become a natural basis for communicating.

Connect with People

The goal of conversation is to connect with people and the world around us. We have much to gain by communicating in an open and mutual manner. By sharing our experiences, we can grow in new ways. Our horizons and opportunities can expand, while our relationships may deepen and become more meaningful. Friendships and a sense of personal fulfillment can develop.

Conversation is also a means of negotiating with others. Communicating our wants and needs effectively is essential to fulfilling them.

Getting Started

Begin by opening your mind and your senses to people and the world around you. Start to integrate your new skills into your personality. You don't have to become a different person; you just need to change your attitudes and skills when you deal with others. Be patient and focus on small daily changes, rather than waiting for revelations. Remember, our patterns have had many years to crystallize, and it takes time for them to change.

You must have the desire to change, reach out to others, and try some new ideas. Set a goal to make contact with others. With a background of basic communication skills, you will find that *accomplishing your goal is easier and more fun than you thought!* So, let's begin and . . . start a conversation!

Part I

Starting Your Conversations with Confidence

Closed body language sends out the message: "Stay away! I'd rather be left alone!"

1

First Contact—
Body Language

It's a luxury to be understood.
—Ralph Waldo Emerson (1803–1882), American poet and essayist

One of our most important conversational skills doesn't come from our tongue, but from our body. Research has shown that over half of face-to-face conversation is nonverbal. "Body language," as it is called, often communicates our feelings and attitudes before we speak, and it projects our level of receptivity to others.

Most poor conversationalists don't realize that their nonreceptive body language (crossed arms, little eye contact, and no smiling) is often the cause of short and unsustained conversations. We are judged quickly by the first signals we give off, and if the first impressions are not open and friendly, it's going to be difficult to maintain a good conversation. The following "softening" techniques can make your first impressions work *for* you, not against you.

S-O-F-T-E-N

A "softener" is a nonverbal gesture that will make people more responsive and receptive to you. Since your body language speaks before you do, it is important to project a receptive image. When you use open body language, you are already sending the signal: "I'm friendly and willing to

"S-O-F-T-E-N" Your Body Language

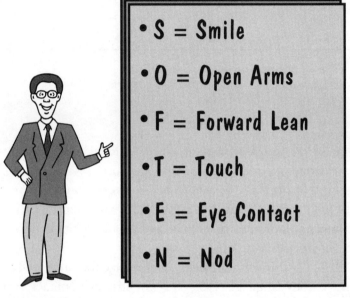

- S = Smile
- O = Open Arms
- F = Forward Lean
- T = Touch
- E = Eye Contact
- N = Nod

Use your body language to break down the natural barriers that separate strangers.

communicate, if you are." Each letter in S-O-F-T-E-N represents a specific nonverbal technique for encouraging others to talk with you.

S = Smile

A pleasant *smile* is a strong indication of a friendly and open attitude and a willingness to communicate. It is a receptive, nonverbal signal sent with the hope that the other person will smile back. When you smile, you demonstrate that you have noticed the person in a positive manner. The other person considers it a compliment and will usually feel good. The result? The other person will usually smile back.

Smiling does not mean that you have to put on a phony face or pretend that you are happy all of the time. But when you see someone you know, or would like to make contact with, do smile. By smiling, you are demonstrating an open attitude to conversation.

The human face sends out an enormous number of verbal and nonverbal signals. If you send out friendly messages, you're going to get friendly messages back. When you couple a warm smile with a friendly hello, you'll be pleasantly surprised by similar responses. It's the easiest and best way to show someone that you've noticed him. A smile indicates general approval toward the other person, and this will usually make the other person feel more open to talk to you.

A smile shows you are friendly and open to communication. When you frown or wrinkle your brow, you give off signals of skepticism and nonreceptivity.

Crossed arms: "I'm thinking and don't want to be disturbed. Stay away!"

Open arms: "I'm receptive and available for contact."

O = Open Arms

The letter *O* in S-O-F-T-E-N stands for *open arms.* You've probably been welcomed with "open arms," which, of course, means that a person was glad to see you. At a party or in another social or business situation, open arms suggests that you are friendly and available for contact. During a conversation, open arms makes others feel that you are receptive and listening.

On the other hand, standing or sitting with your arms crossed makes you appear closed to contact, defensive, and closed-minded. Add a hand covering your mouth (and your smile) or your chin and you are practically in the classic "thinker's pose." Now just ask yourself this question: Are you going to interrupt someone who appears to be deep in thought? Probably not. In addition, crossing your arms tends to make you appear nervous, judgmental, or skeptical—all of which discourage people from approaching you or feeling comfortable while talking to you.

Some people argue that just because they have their arms crossed, it doesn't mean that they are closed to conversation. They say, "I cross my arms because I'm comfortable that way." They may be comfortable, but the problem is that while no one can read minds, they can read body language. Crossed arms say, "Stay away" and "My mind is made up." Open arms say, "I'm available for contact and willing to listen. Come on over and talk to me."

F = Forward Lean

The letter *F* in S-O-F-T-E-N means *forward lean*. Leaning forward slightly while a person is talking to you indicates interest on your part, and shows you are listening to what the person is saying. This is usually taken as a compliment by the other person, and will encourage him to continue talking.

Leaning back gives off signals of disinterest and even boredom.

Leaning forward says: "I'm interested in what you're saying."

Often people will lean back with their hands over their mouth, chin, or behind their head in the "relaxing" pose. Unfortunately, this posture gives off signals of judgment, skepticism, and boredom from the listener. Since most people do not feel comfortable when they think they are being judged, this leaning-back posture tends to inhibit the speaker from continuing.

It's far better to lean forward slightly in a casual and natural way. By doing this, you are saying: "I hear what you're saying, and I'm interested—keep talking!" This usually lets the other person feel that what he is saying is interesting, and encourages him to continue speaking.

Take care not to violate someone's "personal space" by getting too close, too soon. Of course, if the situation calls for it, the closer the better. However, be sensitive to the other person's body language. Remember, there are cultural differences in what constitutes a comfortable distance between strangers engaged in conversation. For more ways to improve your conversations with people from other countries, read chapters 10 and 11.

T = Touch

The letter *T* in S-O-F-T-E-N stands for *touch*. In our culture, the most acceptable form of first contact between two people who are just meeting is a warm handshake. This is usually true when meeting members of the same or opposite sex— and not just in business, but in social situations, too. In nearly every situation, a warm and firm handshake is a safe way of showing an open and friendly attitude toward the people you meet.

Be the first to extend your hand in greeting. Couple this with a friendly "Hi," a nice smile, and your name, and you have made the first step to open the channels of communication between you and the other person.

Some men don't feel right in offering their hand to a woman first. They say they would feel stupid if the woman didn't shake their hand. Emily Post states in the revised edition of her book of etiquette that it is perfectly acceptable for a man to offer a handshake to a woman, and that, in most cases, it would be rude for either man or woman to ignore or refuse this friendly gesture.

A friendly handshake with a smile and a warm "Hello. . . . Nice to meet you" is an easy, acceptable form of touch when meeting someone for the first time.

Some women, on the other hand, feel that they are being too forward if they offer a handshake to a man. They think the man might get the "wrong idea" if they extend their hand first in greeting. The problem is that there are two people who are afraid to shake hands. Although there are some exceptions because of religious customs, most of the people I've polled on the subject agree: no matter who makes the first move, nearly everyone likes this form of physical contact. It's safe and nonthreatening for both parties. This keeps personal defenses down and creates an atmosphere of equality and receptivity between the people. More personal forms of touch should be exercised with a sensitivity to the other person's culture, and in a warm, nonaggressive manner.

It is also important to end your conversations with a warm and friendly handshake, in business as well as social situations. Couple it with a bright smile and a friendly statement like, "I've really enjoyed talking with you!" or "Let's get together again soon!" This is an excellent way to end a conversation and leaves you and the other person both feeling good about the exchange.

E = Eye Contact

The letter *E* in S-O-F-T-E-N represents *eye contact.* Perhaps the strongest of the nonverbal gestures are sent through the eyes. Direct eye contact indicates that you are listening to the other person, and that you want to know about her. Couple eye contact with a friendly smile, and you'll send this unmistakable message: "I'd like to talk to you, and maybe get to know you better."

Eye contact should be natural and not forced or overdone. It is perfectly okay to have brief periods of eye contact while you observe other parts of the person's face—particularly the mouth. When the person smiles, be sure to smile back.

But always make an effort to return your gaze to the person's eyes as she speaks. It is common to look up, down, and all around when speaking to others, and it's acceptable not to have eye contact at all times.

Too much eye contact can be counterproductive. If you stare at a person, she may feel uncomfortable and even suspicious about your intentions. A fixed stare can appear as aggressive behavior if it takes the form of a challenge as to who will look away first. It is not wise to employ eye contact as a "power struggle," because it will usually result in a negative, defensive response from the other person.

If you have a problem maintaining comfortable eye contact, try these suggestions. Start with short periods of eye contact—maybe only a few seconds. Look into the pupils of the other person's eyes, and smile. Then let your gaze travel over the features of her face, hair, nose, lips, and even earlobes! There is a six-inch diameter around the eyes that can provide a visual pathway. Remember, after a few moments, go back to

Eye contact shows that you are listening and taking an interest in what is being said. It sends the signal: "I'm listening—keep talking!"

looking the person right in the eyes. You can look back and forth between both eyes while increasing the amount of time that you experience direct eye contact as the conversation continues.

Avoiding eye contact can make both parties feel anxious and uncomfortable, and can give the impression that you are uninterested, dishonest, or bored with the conversation and the company. The result will usually be a short and unfulfilling conversation. So be sure to look into the eyes of the people you talk with, and send this message: "I hear what you're saying—go on!"

N = Nod

The letter *N* in S-O-F-T-E-N stands for *nod.* A nod of the head indicates that you are listening and that you understand what

A nod of the head shows you are listening and understand what is being said. It sends the message: "I hear you, go on!" A blank stare suggests your thoughts are elsewhere.

is being said. It usually signals approval and encourages the other person to continue talking. A nod of the head, coupled with a smile and a friendly hello, is an excellent way of greeting people on the street, or anywhere else. Like all the other softening gestures, it sends the same message: "I'm friendly and willing to communicate."

However, a nod does not necessarily mean agreement. If you want to be sure someone agrees with what you're saying, ask, "Do you agree?"

Body Language + Tone of Voice + Words = Total Communication

Remember that these nonverbal softening gestures alone do not replace verbal communication. Moreover, if you only see an isolated gesture, rather than clusters of gestures, your perception of the other person's receptivity may be incorrect. However, when you look for and use clusters of these softening gestures together with a friendly tone of voice and inviting words, you will create an impression of openness and availability for contact and conversation.

With practice and a greater awareness of body language, you will be able to send and receive receptive signals, and encourage others to approach you and feel comfortable. Begin to notice other people's body language as well as your own. This will help you to identify softening techniques and recognize levels of receptivity in others, thus minimizing the chance of being rejected. Look for people who display receptive body language and project receptive body language by using softening techniques—they really work!!

Total Communication

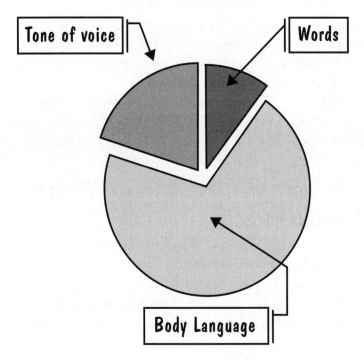

Your body language speaks *before* you do. Research has shown that over two-thirds of face-to-face conversation is based on body language. Along with the tone of your voice and the words you use, they add up to "total communication."

FAQ

I'm at a cocktail party, and I don't know anyone. It seems like everybody knows everybody else, except me. How do I go up to someone and start a conversation?

Starting conversations at a party is easier if you first take a little extra time to prepare mentally. Scan a few current magazines and newspapers for unusual or interesting stories. Look for any news items that may be of interest to other guests you know will be at the party. In addition, write a short list of events going on in your life that you are willing to share with others. Remember, the more "conversational fuel" you bring to the party, the easier it will be to break the ice and get a conversation going.

When you enter the room, look for friendly faces among the crowd and for people talking. You might assume that just because people are having a lively chat, they are old buddies, but often they have just met minutes before, so don't assume you're the only outsider. Use plenty of eye contact, smile, and above all, keep your arms uncrossed and your hands away from your face. Begin to circulate around the room, observing the people as you travel to the food table, bar, or central area where people are congregating and talking. Keep your eyes open for friends, acquaintances, or people already engaged in a conversation that appears open to others. Then casually stroll over and (using their names, if you remember) say, "Hi, how are you?" or "Well, hello! It's been a while. How have you been?" or "Hello, my name is . . ." or "Hi, didn't we meet at . . . ? My name is . . ." Remember, what you say is less important than sending body language signals that say you want to communicate.

When you meet a complete stranger at a party, the easiest way to break the ice is to introduce yourself and say how you know the host. In most cases, the other person will reciprocate. Listen carefully for any words that may suggest a common interest or connection. For example, perhaps you both work for the same business or live in the same neighborhood, but never had the opportunity to formally meet. You can also comment about the food, the music, the pictures on the walls, or anything or anyone in your immediate surroundings—as long as it is positive! Here are some opening lines that will come in handy at a cocktail party.

(To someone beside you at the food table): "I'm wondering, do you have any idea what ingredients are in this appetizer? It's fantastic!"

(To someone tapping her foot to the music): "You look like you're really enjoying this music. Me too. Do you want to dance?"

(To someone who obviously spent extra effort to look really snazzy): "Excuse me, but I couldn't help but notice what an attractive scarf you have on. How did you come up with such an unusual way to tie it?"

(To someone standing alone after a business-related party): "Hello. My name is Sam. Actually, I'm a new member in this organization. What did you think of tonight's speaker?"

(To someone admiring an antique or knickknack): "I love all these old toys and odds and ends. I think our host must like to go to garage sales and flea markets as much as I do. I wonder why so many people love to collect the strangest things."

(To someone dancing): "Excuse me, but you sure look great out there on the dance floor. Would you show me a few steps?"

2

Breaking the Ice and Getting the Conversation Going

> Ideal conversation must be an exchange of thought, and not, as many of those who worry most about their shortcomings believe, an eloquent exhibition of wit or oratory.
>
> —Emily Post (1873–1960), writer and authority on etiquette

So now that you're tuned in to the conversation channel of body language, how do you actually start a conversation? How do you break the ice?

There are five basic steps in starting conversation, which don't always occur in this order. *Establish eye contact and smile,* then follow this simple procedure.

1. *Risk versus rejection.* Be the first to say hello.
2. *Ritual questions.* Ask easy-to-answer questions about the situation or the other person.
3. *Active listening.* Know what to say next by listening carefully for free information.
4. *Seek information.* Ask information-seeking follow-up questions based on free information *you've just heard.*
5. *Self-disclosure.* Reveal plenty of your free information while asking questions that may interest you personally.

Four Ways to Start Conversations

Ask a closed-ended or open-ended question

Make a positive or light-hearted comment

Offer a compliment followed by an easy-to-answer question

Introduce yourself

Changing topics is easy if you say, "I heard you mention earlier. . . ." or "Speaking of. . . ." Then ask a question or share information about a general or specific topic related to key words you hear.

1. Risk Versus Rejection

It takes a certain amount of risk to begin a conversation with a stranger. Most shy people don't start conversations because they fear being rejected. Of course, this prevents them from reaching out to others. Remember that risk taking and rejection are part of life, and to be overly sensitive is counterproductive. And, anyway, what's so bad about being rejected by someone you don't even know?

Change from Passive to Active

Most shy people take the passive role when it comes to starting conversations. They wait and wait and wait, hoping someone will come along and start a conversation with them. If there are two shy people together, they're both waiting, both taking the passive role. If someone else by chance does start talking, the shy person is often so surprised, she doesn't know what to say.

To get out of this "Catch-22," consciously change from the passive to the active role. Be the first to say hello and take the initiative to begin the conversation. Introduce yourself to people regularly and begin to share your ideas, feelings, opinions, and experiences. Look for familiar faces, and after saying hello, seek out other people's thoughts, views, interests, and knowledge. By initiating conversations, you'll get more positive responses, and your fear of rejection will lessen. In this way your risk taking can pay off in making new contacts and having more meaningful conversations.

Another advantage of being the first to say hello is that it gives you the opportunity to guide the direction of the conversation, and gives the other person the impression that you are confident, friendly, and open. You are also complimenting the other person by showing a desire to start a conversation with him.

Minimize Rejections—Look for Receptivity

The more you practice starting conversations, the better responses you will get. But, of course, there are going to be some rejections too. No one receives unanimous approval, so when you do get rejected, don't dwell on it. Instead, use it as a lesson and adjust your approach for next time.

The best way to minimize rejection is to look for receptivity in those you approach. Try to be sensitive to "where others are at." Look for open arms, eye contact, and a smile. Look for people who are sending receptive signals through their body language, and when you feel the time is right, approach them in a friendly and direct way. For example, if you are at a party or dance, and would like to ask someone for a dance, then look to those who either are dancing or look like they want to dance. Wait for a new song to start playing, and then take the risk. Move closer to the person and establish eye contact, smile, and ask the person for a dance. Chances are she will feel flattered that you have noticed her and hopefully will accept your invitation. If, however, the answer is no, then accept it gracefully with a smile (like water off a duck's back), and ask someone else. Keep asking and you're bound to get an acceptance. The more you ask, the better you'll get at picking out people who will respond the way you want them to.

How to Accept Rejections

If you have been rejected many times in your life, then one more rejection isn't going to make much difference. If you're rejected, don't automatically assume it's your fault. The other person may have several reasons for not doing what you are asking him to do; none of it may have anything to do with you. Perhaps the person is busy or not feeling well or genuinely not interested in spending time with you. Rejections are a part of everyday life. Don't let them keep you from reaching out to others. When you begin to get encouraging responses, then you are on the right track. It's all a matter of numbers. Count the positive responses and forget about the rejections.

This simple philosophy can help people who fear rejection. If you have only taken a few social risks and have been rejected once or twice, then those rejections loom very large in your life. If, on the other hand, you take more risks, and start conversations, you will receive a mixture of open and closed responses, and each rejection will become less and less meaningful. Focus on the positive responses, and you will get better at choosing receptive people.

You really have very little to lose, and a lot to gain. Taking the risk to be the first to say hello isn't such a fearful step. When you take the active role, you are sending this message: "I'm friendly and willing to communicate if you are."

2. Ask Easy-to-Answer Ritual Questions

Ritual questions are easy-to-answer requests for information. Although basically requests for personal background or general information, they also convey this message: "I'm interested in getting to know you better."

Breaking the Ice—A Compliment or Comment Followed by a Ritual Question

Ritual questions can be used to break the ice with someone you don't know and wish to speak to. The easiest way to start a conversation with a stranger is to employ one of the three following openings. First, notice something interesting about the person you wish to speak with and, in a friendly and sincere manner, offer a compliment. Quickly follow the compliment with a ritual question that is directly related to the compliment you just gave. The "opening line" might be: "That's a beautiful ring you're wearing! What kind of stone is it?" or "Say, you're a terrific skater! How did you learn to do all those tricks?"

A second way to break the ice is to notice something that the person is carrying—maybe a book, musical instrument, or a piece of sporting equipment. After establishing eye contact and smiling, ask a ritual question based on the object. For example, if you see someone carrying a tennis racket, you could say something like: "Excuse me, but could you recommend a good place to take tennis lessons?" or "Do you know a good place to play without having to wait for a court?" or "I notice you have a racket like the one I'm interested in buying. How do you like it?" or "I see you're a tennis player. I want to start playing. Can you recommend a good racket for a beginner?"

If you see someone reading or carrying a book, you can ask how he likes it. If a person has a musical instrument, you can ask him what kind of music he plays, where he plays or studies, how long he has been playing, or how you might get involved. If you see someone taking photographs, you could ask him about the type of camera he has or if he is a professional or amateur photographer. These questions can be applied to almost any object a person is carrying. It is a safe and friendly way of showing someone you've noticed him, while breaking the ice and starting a conversation at the same time.

A third way to break the ice and start a conversation is to make a comment or ask a question based on the situation.

A compliment followed by an easy-to-answer ritual question is a good way to break the ice.

This can be a request for information like: "Say, excuse me, but I'm looking for an apartment in the neighborhood. Do you happen to know of any places that might be for rent?" Another common question might be: "I'm looking for a good place to eat nearby. Can you recommend a restaurant in the neighborhood?" If you see someone who looks like she needs some assistance, then offering to help is an excellent way to start a conversation. You might say: "You look a little lost. Are you looking for someplace in particular? I live in the neighborhood—maybe I can help you."

In addition to asking for or offering assistance, another way to start a conversation is to make comments based on what you observe. It is best to focus on the positive things you see rather than complaining about the negative. This way you can let others in on the way you see the world, and not get caught in a conversation of "Ain't it a shame!" If you happen to be standing in a movie line, you can comment on other films, or the most recent book you've read if you are browsing in a bookstore. A straight-forward comment you can make is: "I've seen you here before. Do you live or work around here?"

Ritual questions are good for breaking the ice and starting a conversation. By looking for what people are involved in, you can easily focus on a topic of interest to the other person. Remember, in addition to finding out about the other person, you are sending this signal: "You seem interesting to me, and I'd like to get to know you better!"

FAQ

I dine at a local restaurant where I often see someone else who usually eats alone. How can I ask her if she wants to join me for dinner?

Make an effort to be seated near the person dining alone, and when she looks in your direction, make eye contact, nod, and smile. If she smiles back, you can say, "Hello. I've noticed that you eat here a lot, too. What's for dinner tonight?" Remember that you are just showing interest and seeing if she appears open for contact. If her response is friendly, you might say, "I really like their sandwiches here, but tonight I feel like something different. What do you usually order?" The goal is to start a conversation from your separate seats and see where it leads. If it seems like she wants to continue to talk you can say, "If you're not waiting for someone, would you like to join me?" or "Do you mind if I join you?"

Many people who frequently dine alone might be happy to accept your invitation if you approach them in a friendly and low-pressured way. You can also offer to buy a person a drink to show you are interested in chatting with her. Just remember that your offer is only a friendly gesture and doesn't necessarily mean that you are treating her to dinner or that she owes you anything in return. However, if she declines your invitation, she may be shy or she might simply prefer her own company. Don't get upset or angry. Just smile and say, "No problem, enjoy your meal."

The Perfect Time to Introduce Yourself

Exchanging ritual information also allows you to prepare to introduce yourself to the other person. Generally, the longer you wait to make an introduction, the more uncomfortable people get, so the sooner you take the initiative, the better. When there is a pause in conversation, this is a good time to say, "By the way, my name is . . . What's yours?" The other person will almost certainly respond in kind. Offer a handshake and a friendly smile, and say: "Nice to meet you." Then ask a question or make a comment about what the other person has told you, and your conversation will be off and running.

Closed and Open Ritual Questions

You might find yourself asking ritual question after ritual question, and only getting one- or two-word answers. This is probably because you are asking "closed-ended" ritual questions instead of "open-ended" ritual questions.

Closed-ended ritual questions usually require only a yes or a no, or just a one- or two-word answer. They are "fishing questions" because you're looking for a "bite." Closed-ended

Ask Closed & Open-ended Questions

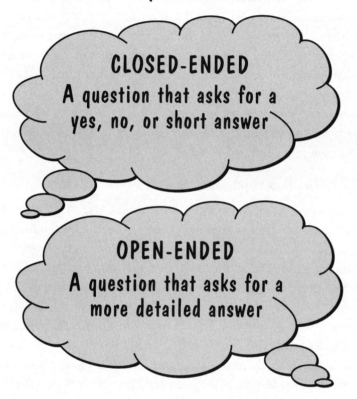

questions are useful for breaking the ice and finding out some basic facts, but they are more effective when followed with an open-ended question. *Open-ended* ritual questions usually require a more detailed answer, and they encourage the other person to talk. In addition, they provide an opportunity to reveal facts, opinions, feelings, and most important, plenty of free information. Closed-ended questions often begin with words like: Are? Do? Who? Where? and Which? Open-ended ritual questions commonly start with How?

Why? In what way? How did you get involved? How can I get involved? "What" can be used as both an open- and closed-ended question.

Here are some common examples of closed-ended ritual questions.

Do you live around here?
Do you like the food?
What time is it?
Are you going to the park?
When did you get here?
Where are you from?
Are you enjoying your stay here?
Is this your first visit here?

Here are some examples of *open-ended* ritual questions.

How did you find your apartment?
In what ways do you think this country (city, college, etc.) has changed?
How did you get involved in that line of work?
Why did you decide to move there?
What brings you to our town?
What do you like to do on your days off?

These are just a few examples of closed- and open-ended ritual questions. Remember to follow closed questions with open-ended questions. In this way you can fish for topics of interest and then seek further information by asking open-ended questions.

Make your questions easy and straightforward. Most people are far more comfortable answering expected, easy-to-answer questions when they first meet a person, rather than difficult or complicated questions that put them on the spot.

Some people think that they may offend the other person if they ask ritual questions. They say they don't want to be too personal or pry. In most cases, the opposite is true. Most people feel flattered when someone notices them in a friendly way and shows a genuine interest. This usually encourages the person to talk.

It is also very important that you be willing to answer ritual questions. Answering a closed-ended question with more than just a one- or two-word answer shows that you are willing to talk. Your extended answer also offers the other person more information to ask you about or an opportunity for him or her to share a related experience. For example, let's say someone you've just met asks you a closed-ended question like, "Where are you from?" You can answer, "I grew up in . . . , but I've been living in . . . and working as a . . . for the last five years."

Free Information

When we communicate with one another, we reveal much more than we realize. The information that we volunteer is called *free information*. When you ask or answer a ritual question, be aware of the free information that accompanies the answer. Focus on this, and use it as conversational fuel for follow-up questions. By focusing on the free information we can explore each other's experiences and interests in a natural and free-flowing manner.

Telling Others What You Do

Some people feel uncomfortable if others ask them the ritual question "What do you do?" They feel people will stereotype them or make assumptions based on how they earn a living. No one likes being put into a pigeonhole, but if you get angry or become resistant when asked about your profession, you'll throw cold water on the conversation. Although it may not be a good first question to ask when you meet someone, being ready with a short answer is useful.

If you like talking about your profession, then reveal some free information and see if the other person shows more interest. After a few sentences about your line of work, it's fine to ask what he or she does for a living. For example, you can say, "So now you know a little about what I do for work. What about you?" If, however, you prefer not to discuss your work, still answer the question in a word or two. Then add free information about what you do want to talk about. For example, you might say, "To pay the bills I work as an attorney for a bank, but my real passion is French cooking!"

You can reveal other basic facts about yourself, while guiding the direction of the conversation. If you insist on not disclosing this information, the other party will slowly become suspicious (especially if he has given out that information) or lose interest in trying to get to know you. If you expect to be friends with this person, how long can you withhold this basic information?

Many people who don't like to tell others what they do are also anxious about other types of ritual questions. They feel small talk is dull and boring, and should be avoided. Instead, they say they want to talk about something important.

While there isn't a particular order as to how conversations should proceed, most conversations that do not go through the "ritual" phases rarely proceed to deeper and more meaningful levels. Small talk is a very important element in conversations and in establishing friendships and relationships.

The Power of Small Talk

Small talk often gets a bad rap, but it is one of the most useful communication tools we have. Small talk encourages conversation because it:

1. Demonstrates a willingness to talk.
2. Allows people to exchange basic information and find common interests.
3. Provides an opportunity for speakers to reveal the topics that they want to talk about.

Getting to Know You

Ritual questions allow you to reveal basic personal information in a natural and informal way. By exchanging little details about one another, you can get to know the person you are talking with very quickly. Ritual questions help you quickly determine if you would like to get to know this person better. Ritual questions help you to find out and disclose personal backgrounds, and provide an opportunity to discover the "big things" in a person's life.

Ask ritual questions when you want to break the ice or change topics in conversation. If your ritual question gets a brief response, try another until you get an enthusiastic response. When you discover an area of interest in the other person, be sure to follow with an open-ended information-seeking question. When the topic seems to be running out of steam (you don't have to talk a subject completely out), return to another ritual question based on free information that you or the other person revealed earlier.

If you employ these ritual question techniques for breaking the ice with the people you meet, you'll discover they really do work. Being the first to say hello won't be a problem any longer.

3. Know What to Say by Listening (Active Listening)

Okay, so you ask a few ritual questions, then what do you say? You always seem to run out of things to talk about in less than a minute! You can never think of what to say next!

Don't Think—Listen for "Key Words"!

Know what to say next by listening carefully for key words, facts, opinions, feelings, and most of all, free information. Don't think about what you are going to say next, because while you are thinking, you're not listening! Most shy people are usually so preoccupied with—"Oh no, it's going to be my turn to talk soon, and I won't know what to say!"—that they don't hear what the other person is saying.

The solution to this problem is to use *active listening skills* while the other person is speaking. These include using good body language, especially eye contact, smiling, and nodding in response. Active listening encourages people to continue speaking, and it shows that your attention is focused on the conversation.

Improve Your Listening Skills

Conversation problems include poor listening, memory, and concentration skills. There is usually enough time for your mind to wander while you are being spoken to, and many

Use and Listen for "Key Words"

KEY WORDS			
PEOPLE	**PLACES**	**THINGS**	**ACTIVITIES**
Family	Home	Cars	Hobbies
Friends	School	Clothes	Fitness
Coworkers	Workplace	Computers	Recreation
Relationships	Neighborhood	Books	Education
Acquaintances	Cities	Tools	Volunteer work
Teachers	Countries	Musical instruments	Profession
Political leaders	Parks	Electronics	Entertainment
Mentors	House of worship	Sports equipment	Vacations

people speak slowly and with lengthy pauses between thoughts. The result is that your mind may wander. You can lose your concentration and even the main idea of the conversation.

Ask Relevant Follow-up Questions

Asking relevant follow-up questions based on what the other person has said shows you are listening. Closed-ended questions help to clarify facts and details. Open-ended questions encourage the speaker to elaborate and suggest that you are interested in the topic.

Use Examples

Ask for and think of examples that support or question what is being said. If you are not sure what the other person is saying, or you don't understand what she is talking about, ask for an example to make the point clear for you.

Anticipate

A good listener is actively involved in the conversation, and can often anticipate what the speaker is going to say next. This involvement shows concern and interest, and will usually reinforce facts and details. If you anticipated the speaker correctly, then you know you are probably on the same wavelength. If your anticipations were not correct, this can be a warning signal that you and your partner are not tuned in to each other, and that a misunderstanding may be developing. *Caution:* Don't finish the other person's sentences. Not only is it rude, it shows you're not listening.

Summarize

It is not uncommon for people talking to wander off the main topic. When you are listening, it is helpful to keep the main theme in mind, and from time to time, summarize what the other person has said. You can say something like: "It sounds to me like you are saying . . . Am I right?" This focuses your listening skills, and helps you remember important details and the main ideas of the conversation. When you understand her main point, restate it. For example, you can say, "If I understand you correctly, you think . . ."

Get Actively Involved

Conversations are more fun when you get actively involved. By participating, you'll improve your listening skills and retention of details and main ideas. Plus, the other person will feel more comfortable because you're showing interest in what he has been talking about. Be sure to link the new information with your prior knowledge and experience. Ask yourself: "How does what he just said relate to my understanding and experience of the topic?" Combining your prior knowledge and new information will provide you with enough new questions and comments to easily continue the conversation.

Listen for "Iceberg" Statements

An "iceberg" statement is a comment or a piece of free information where 90 percent is under the surface, waiting to be asked about. Iceberg statements usually come in the form of one or two words that accompany answers to ritual questions. These statements are hints about topics that the person really wants to talk about if she thinks you might be interested. When you hear an iceberg statement like, "You'll never believe what happened to me . . ." or "Guess what I've been doing," quickly ask a related follow-up question or say: "What happened?" or "You don't say! Tell me, how was it?" Other follow-up open-ended questions are "Why do you say that?" "In what ways?" and "How so?"

FAQ

How do I enter a conversation at a networking event when two or three people are talking to each other?

To enter a conversation in progress, you must be within listening and speaking range. Move close to the people speaking and show interest in what is being said. Use plenty of eye contact, nodding, and smiling to send the signal to the

Listen for "Iceberg Statements"

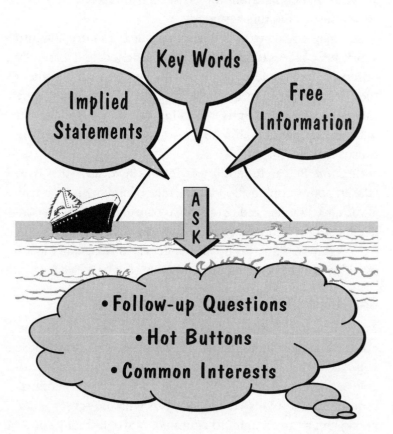

speaker that you want to hear more. Often, when a speaker sees you are interested in what he is saying, he will begin to include you as a listener.

When there is a pause, or the speaker says something you can respond to, then interject your comment or question into the conversation. If you use easy-to-answer information questions, the answers will be directed to you specifically. Say something like, "What did you do then?" or "How did you arrive at that conclusion?" or "That's a truly incredible story! How long ago did this happen?"

You may be saying to yourself that this is an intrusion into a private conversation. If you have listened and carefully observed the people, you will quickly be able to determine if they are receptive. In many cases, especially at networking functions, the speaker is searching for others to interact with, and a new person who shows interest in participating is usually welcome.

Caution: Be careful not to play devil's advocate—that is, to take an opposition position for the sake of argument. This usually leads to a tense and competitive conversation, with a winner and a loser. You won't be considered a welcome addition to a conversation with a group of strangers if you make them look stupid or embarrassed in front of their friends or colleagues.

Good Listening Requires Practice and Concentration

Active listening skills need to be practiced and will aid your conversational abilities immensely. They will encourage those you talk with to elaborate further and to feel more comfortable in opening up to you. When you share a person's enthusiasm for a topic by listening closely to what he says, you are giving him a "green light" to continue. Active listening shows your interest and curiosity in a person by sending this message: "I'm interested in what you are saying—keep talking, I want to hear more!"

4. Seek More Information Based on Free Information

After you have broken the ice, asked a few ritual questions, and used active listening, then seek further information based on the free information you have learned. By taking advantage of free information, you can guide the direction of the conversation. Ask open-ended questions that refer to the free information either you or your conversation partner has revealed.

Free information is communicated by a person's clothing, physical features, body language, personal behavior, and activities, as well as by her words. Sometimes free information will consist of a general impression. Then you can say something like: "You seem to know a lot about _____. Are you involved with _____?" or "You sound like an expert. Do you teach a class on that subject?" or "That laptop you're using sure looks cool. What kind is it?"

Always try to follow closed-ended ritual questions with an open-ended ritual question, to give your partner a chance to elaborate on the topic. For example, "What made you decide to buy that model?" Pay close attention to facts, details, and especially more free information, with the idea of directing the conversation into areas of mutual interest.

When discussing areas of professional interest, take care not to "pick the person's brain." Don't ask for free advice on a particular problem you are having. For example, if you meet a dentist, DON'T say: "Oh, you're a dentist! How convenient! Say, I've got this sore tooth here, and I was wondering, as long as we are here, would you take a look?" Most professionals don't mind telling others what they do, and even discussing their work if they think you are interested, but they resent being hit up for a free office visit.

Asking Personal Questions

Asking personal questions always requires a particular sensitivity to the other person's feelings, and especially his level of receptivity to you. It is usually best to preface personal questions with a softener like, "Excuse me for asking but . . ." or

"I'd love to know, if you don't mind telling me . . . ?" or "I hope I'm not being too personal, but . . . ?" or "If you don't mind my asking . . . ?"

If you ask a personal question in such a way that the other person does not have to answer, often he will respond in some form. It may not be the direct answer you are looking for, because many people have trouble saying what they really mean, especially it it's about a sensitive topic. However, if you listen carefully for free information and look for receptive body language, you can get an idea about whether the person trusts you enough to reveal some personal information.

FAQ

How do you gracefully tell someone she is asking questions that are too personal?

If you are asked a question you'd rather not answer, simply say, "I'd rather not answer that question, if you don't mind." Most people will accept this statement as a courteous way of saying, "Mind your own business." If you are asked how much something costs and you'd rather not discuss it, say "I don't really know because it was a gift," or you can say with a wink, "Too much" or "Not enough."

A word of caution: Many people are overly concerned about revealing certain ritual information such as their occupation, where they are from, etc. Don't be resistant about answering these "signals of interest" ritual questions.

If you feel a question is too personal to answer, or you'd rather not, it is your right to do as you wish. After declining to answer, throw the conversational ball back to the other person with a ritual question on a new topic.

Disclose your hopes, dreams, loves, joys, and sorrows so people will be able to identify with you. We all share these basic emotional experiences.

Avoid Pitfalls When Seeking Information

Avoid traditional conversational taboos such as death, gory crimes, unhappy events, personal gossip, or racial and ethnic slurs. Avoid getting things off your chest and using the other person to tell all your troubles to. It is best not to overdramatize regular daily events in your life or call attention to problems that your conversational partner cannot easily solve. These interactions can create a negative impression about you. Remember that it's better to begin with easy questions that are upbeat. They will encourage your partner to feel comfortable and allow you both to get to know each other through gradual self-disclosure.

Listen carefully for topics a person may wish to avoid discussing. Be sensitive to the other person's feelings, and don't make him just answer question after question if you get the feeling he'd rather not talk about a particular subject or issue. A "cross-examination" can turn the other person off and usually occurs when you ask too many closed-ended ritual questions.

5. Disclose Free Information

Self-disclosure completes the conversational cycle of taking risks, asking ritual questions, active listening, and seeking information.

It's a Way to Let Others Get to Know You

Self-disclosure lets others get to know you on your own terms. The information you share with the people you meet determines how they get to know you. Be enthusiastic when you share your personal interests and the "big" events in your life, including your hopes, goals, and most rewarding experiences. You can gradually tell others what you do for employment, your background, goals, and, most important, your availability for future contact.

To Tell or Not to Tell—That Is the Question

Do you maintain a veil of privacy because you believe that: 1) if people knew what you were really like, they would think less of you; 2) being too familiar with someone breeds contempt, so remaining mysterious is best; or 3) if a person knew intimate or personal facts about you, she might use this information against you?

Yes, a certain amount of caution about revealing personal aspects of one's past is prudent. However, if you are secretive, you will leave the impression that you have something to hide. No one expects (or wants) you to reveal your deepest fears or secrets, but if you desire meaningful conversations, be prepared to reveal some of your history and what is important to you.

Realistically, What Do You Have to Lose?

People who resist disclosing personal information place much more importance on it than the details warrant. Once you take a look at what is being revealed, the details aren't secrets that must be kept. Close and meaningful relationships are nearly impossible without personal revelations and mutual trust and confidence. Trust is created by being willing to reveal some personal information to the other person. While some feelings are best kept to oneself, especially in work-related situations, it can be destructive to let this guarded attitude carry over into your personal life. Although there are people who do take unfair advantage of others' personal disclosures, avoiding sharing personal feelings is a guarantee of a life of loneliness and isolation.

To overcome this problem, begin to observe others as they disclose information to you and others. See how often you bury your feelings and opinions. Take the risk of being more open with your disclosures. The next time someone asks you a question about your background, personal feelings, or opinions, remember you are entitled to think and feel as you please. You are free to express yourself to others.

Self-Disclosure—Four Levels to Building Trust

There are four levels of self-disclosure that we use daily. The first is called "cliché" greeting. These are very general disclosures and are responses to ritual greetings such as: "How are you?" "What's new?" "How are you doing?" "How have you been?" or "How's the family?" Though these questions evoke responses such as "Fine!" or "Just great, couldn't be better," they provide an excellent opportunity to reveal free information. These low-level disclosures tell the other person that your attitude is open and friendly, and if the situation permits, that you are available for conversation.

After people exchange greetings, they usually exchange some basic personal facts. Tell others what you do, where you are from, what you like to do for fun, or some current project or activity that you are involved in. This second level of self-disclosure provides a background of experiences and information for conversational partners to compare and explore. It is at this point that people begin to get to know one another.

The third level of self-disclosure is revealing personal opinions and preferences on different subjects. At this level you can reveal your attitudes, values, and concerns. You can tell others what you honestly think and feel about the world around us. Express your ideas in an open manner and encourage others to share their ideas on varied topics. Remember, people have differing views. Good conversation is *not a debate,* with a winner and a loser, but an exchange of views and ideas. Open-minded discussion, not arguing, is an excellent means of sustaining a conversation while letting the participants know more about one another on a more meaningful level.

The final level of self-disclosure is your personal feelings—especially about the people you know and wish to become closer to. These are the most difficult disclosures for most people to make because they require revealing our emotions. Though it can be difficult (and risky) to reveal your feelings, it will give your partners a more meaningful sense of who you are, and what is important to you. When you disclose your hopes, dreams, loves, joys, and sorrows, people will be able to identify with you, because we all share these basic emotional experiences. Many people make the common mistake of using the word "you" when they mean "I." When you disclose your feelings and opinions, remember to use the words "I feel (think, believe," etc.).

Helpful Self-Disclosure Hints

Be Careful About How Much You Disclose

Don't go to the opposite extreme of "telling all." We've all had the experience of someone telling us her life story—and we know how uncomfortable this can be. It's better to reveal your background and ideas a little at a time and within the context of the conversation.

Be Realistic About Yourself

If you exaggerate your good qualities and hide your faults, people will soon realize that you are not presenting a real picture. It's important to *be yourself.* Sometimes people won't believe what you tell them, so disclose specific details including names, dates, and places. Let the discussion continue along with your self-disclosures so that you're certain your partner is taking you seriously.

Reveal Your Goals

Reveal your goals and struggles. You'll be surprised to learn that most people empathize with you and will usually be encouraging. The person you are talking with may be able to assist you in some way. By the same token, you may be able to assist your partner with his goals. If you can help someone else, you're certain to make a friend right away!

Let Someone Get to Know You

Don't be afraid of boring the other person. Most people are interested in making new friends, and it's essential to let others know who you are and if you have mutual interests. *You don't have to entertain the people you meet,* but be as upbeat as possible. Most people value personal contact. When you share aspects of your life with another person, you are making this all-important contact with her.

The following sample dialogue identifies the four levels of self-disclosure.

(greeting)	D: Hi, Bonnie! How are you?
(greeting)	B: Oh, hi, Don. I've been pretty good. What have you been up to?
(fact/preference)	D: Busy writing books and presenting workshops, plus I've been gardening in my spare time. What about you?
(fact/preference)	B: I'm still in sales, but I want to do something new. I'd like a job where I can use my computer graphic skills.
(opinion)	I think it's important to work at something you enjoy, don't you?
(opinion)	D: I couldn't agree more. So are you actively looking for a job?

(fact)	B: I've sent my résumé to several companies in the area.
(preference)	I'm hoping to find a job near where I live so I can walk or ride my bike to work.
(opinion)	D: That's a good idea. I think walking is a great way to exercise. All you need is a good pair of walking shoes.
(feeling)	B: I feel more relaxed after I exercise and it helps me concentrate on my work.
(opinion)	I wish businesses would encourage their employees to get more exercise.
(fact)	D: I walk to the post office every day. It's only about a mile round trip,
(opinion)	but I think it helps me work, too.
(feeling)	Besides, I enjoy chatting with friendly neighbors like you!
(feeling)	B: That's nice of you to say, Don. You're a good neighbor, too!
(fact)	Well, I guess I'd better get going. I've got a job interview this afternoon and
(feeling)	I'm a little nervous. Happy gardening!
(opinion)	D: I'm sure you'll do great. See you later, Bonnie, and good luck with your interview.

3

Five Seconds to Success: The Art of Remembering Names

> Most people are too conscious of their own problems in this matter to hold yours against you. Even if they wanted to give you a black mark, they wouldn't know next to whose name to put it.
> —Judith Martin, a.k.a. "Miss Manners," author, etiquette expert

Five Seconds to Success

Five seconds! That's all the time you have to make a great first impression. Five seconds is all the time it takes to introduce yourself and remember a person's name. Five seconds! What faster way is there to begin a successful business or social relationship?

The famous author and public speaker Dale Carnegie said, "The sweetest sound in any language is a person's name." There's no question about it. People feel flattered when you remember their names. When you remember the name of a person you've recently met, you make him feel important and special and you add a large measure of personal warmth and friendliness to the conversation. Remembering names also shows that you are listening, builds rapport with new acquaintances, and helps overcome the natural barriers that separate strangers.

A Good Memory for Names Is Rare

How many times have you been talking to someone you've met before—maybe even more than once—and you can't remember his name? Or you're introducing mutual friends or acquaintances, and one person's name just slips right out of your head? Or you go to a party and you are introduced to someone, and five seconds later you can't recall her name? Or maybe you see a client, and you don't remember his name, so it's difficult to introduce him to your boss? As a result of your poor memory, you feel embarrassed and avoid people you already know, as well as new acquaintances because you might offend them by forgetting their names.

Why Do We Forget People's Names?

The most common reason for forgetting names is failing to focus on the moment of introduction, so you never hear them in the first place. You are too busy thinking about what you're going to say next or worrying about what others will think of you. This counterproductive self-talk sounds like this: "What am I going to say after I say hello?" "Does my hair look okay?" "I don't want to be too forward." "I'm sure I'll say something stupid." "I hope I'm making a good impression." "I wonder if . . ."

Other distractions such as loud music or people talking can also cause you to miss the name. But lack of interest is the worst reason for failing to focus on someone's name. If you say to yourself, "I'll probably never see this person again, so why should I bother learning his name," you have set the stage for a disjointed, impersonal, and short conversation.

Five Seconds to Success

Use the following 5-second strategy to remember first names:

🕐 The first second: Focus on the moment of introduction.

🕐 The second second: Don't think about what to say—listen for the name.

🕐 The third second: Repeat the name aloud.

🕐 The fourth second: Think of someone you know with the same name.

🕐 The fifth second: Use the name during and at the end of the conversation.

🕐 The First Second: Focus on the Moment of Introduction

Let the other person know that you consider her name important by giving her your full attention when you are introduced. Make direct eye contact, offer a warm smile, and extend a firm, friendly handshake. Holding on to the other person's hand an extra second can help you focus on the critical moment of introduction and what is about to come next—her name.

🕐 The Second Second: Don't Think about What to Say—Listen for the Name

This is the moment you've been waiting for, so don't blow it by thinking about yourself and what you're going to say next. Concentrate your complete attention and listen for every letter in the person's name, particularly the first initial. If you missed the name, simply say, "Sorry, I didn't catch your name."

Or, "Excuse me, I missed your name." If the name is unusual, a foreign name, or you're still not sure what he has said, ask: "Can you spell your name for me? I want to be sure to get it right."

⊖ The Third Second: Repeat the Name Aloud

Be sure to repeat the name to make sure that you got it right. Quickly imagine the first initial etched on the person's forehead or connect it with a feature on his face. This may sound weird, but it works, especially when you are trying to recall the name later.

Repeating the name also has several additional benefits. First, it lets the other person know that you listened and that you are making a concentrated effort to remember her name. This is flattering. Second, if you got the name wrong, it allows the other person to correct you. Finally, by repeating the name, you think it, say it, and then hear it again, thus giving yourself three more repetitions in addition to hearing the name the first time. And, as most memory experts agree, repetition is one of the key ingredients to retention and recall—or, practice makes perfect.

⊙ The Fourth Second: Think of Someone You Know With the Same Name

Just think of all the people you know named John, Susan, Robert, Diane, Linda, Steve, Mary, or Frank. Chances are good that when you meet someone new, he or she will have the same name as someone you already know, and this will help you remember the name.

As you are introduced, think of someone else you know with the same name—a relative, classmate, or even a pet! It's best to lock in on the *first* person who comes to mind and to use that *same* person each time you meet someone new with that name. For example, each time you meet a new Barbara, always think of Aunt Barbara. The two people don't need to look anything alike. And you don't even need to actually know them personally. The name could belong to a movie star or someone you've heard of (even a cartoon character) but don't know personally. For example, when you meet an Elizabeth, you might think of Elizabeth Taylor or Queen Elizabeth. Michael Jordan may be the first Michael you think of when you meet someone with that name, and so on. This technique may sound strange, but with a little practice, you'll remember most of your new acquaintances with common first names.

⊙ The Fifth Second: Use the Name During and at the End of the Conversation

"Pat, when you said that you . . ." "John, what made you decide to . . . ?" "Eileen, it was really great hearing about your trip to . . ." "James, how can I get in touch with you?"

Using a person's name personalizes the conversation as it reinforces your memory and ability to recall it at your next meeting. Ending the conversation with her name leaves a great first impression and completes the cycle of starting, continuing, and ending a conversation.

The Trick to Remembering Names in a Group

Nearly everyone has been in the situation where there is barely enough time to shake hands with one person before being introduced to someone else. In many cases, there is less than a second or two between introductions. How can you possibly remember everyone's name? It's easy! If you focus on the moment of introduction to each person and then make a "letter chain," you will be able to remember everyone in the group.

Here's how letter chains work. English is filled with many abbreviations, acronyms, company logos using letters, and short words. The trick is to take the first letter of each person's name and quickly hook them together into either an abbreviation, letter logo, short word, or a series of letters. The chances are good that if you can remember one or two of the names, you can use the letter chain to help recall the other people's names as well. Consider the following examples:

Let's say you are at a party and you are introduced to George and Maria. Think "GM," as in General Motors, or "MG," as in the English sports car. If you remember George's name, and you remember "GM" or "MG," that's probably all you'll need to help you recall Maria's name. Suppose you are seated around a table in a restaurant and you're introduced to Theresa, Alba, and Gary. The letter chain is a short word: T-A-G. Look for letter combinations such as brands, logos, abbreviations, call letters of television or radio stations, double letters (they could be the same names), or letters next to each other in the alphabet. For example, Alan, Barbara, and Carlos = A-B-C; Pamela, Harold, and Della = P-H-D; Christine, Nancy, and Nick = C-N-N; Peter and Pat = P-P; Steve and Tom = S-T.

To remember their names, just link the people together, even if they are not sitting or standing next to each other. Letters can be combined in any sequence that helps you give an order to the names and triggers recall. During a free moment, repeat the letters and their corresponding names to yourself a few more times. The more you repeat the names, the stronger they will stick in your mind. If you can think of a better association to fit the group of names, then make it.

Alternate Methods for Remembering Names

A note before you begin making name associations: Don't worry or edit yourself if you think of an unflattering or even downright insulting word association with the person's name. Most people won't ask you how you remembered their names; they'll just feel flattered that you did. If someone does ask, you can simply say, "You really impressed me!" Here are five more ways to remember the names of the people you meet.

"Rhymes With . . ."

Associating a word that rhymes with the name is a fun way to help you recall someone you've just met. For example: Tall or Small Paul, Curly Shirley, Curt the Flirt, Handy Sandy/Andy, Fancy Nancy, Dan the Man, Silly Billy, Witty Kitty, and so on.

First Names That Sound Like Action Words

Some names sound like physical movements, motions, or gestures. Here are a few examples: Phillip, as in Fill Up my gas tank. Eileen, as in I Lean on a post. Carol, as in Christmas Carol. Bob, as in Bobbing for apples. Rob, as in Robber.

First Names That Sound Like Objects

Some first names are the same as objects or words that we see and use every day. Jack, Bell, Rose, Iris, Bill, Jean, Ray, Barry (bury), Art, Angel, Bea (bee), Hope, May, and June are examples of this.

First Names with the Same Initial as a Personal Interest

The first letter of some first names correspond to the first initial of the person's interest. For example, Greg the Guitarist,

Ruth the Runner, Terry the Teacher, Sally the Sailor, or Eleanor the Engineer.

Choose a Feature and Associate It with the Name

Here's another way to remember a name. Look at the person's face carefully, and chances are you will see that one feature stands out. It may be her eyes, nose, ears, chin, forehead, brows, birthmark, hair, or even the shape of her face. For example, Julie's big sparkling eyes make you think of Jewel Julie. Sam's knitted brow makes him look sad, so you think Sad Sam. Frank's heavy eyebrows remind you of two Coney Island hot dogs, so you think Frankfurter Frank. Tim's slim frame makes you think of Tiny Tim. Sandy's black hair makes you think of the black sand beach in Hawaii, so you think Black Hair like Sand Sandy. Some other possibilities are Bushy Bearded Bill, Muscular Mark, Large Larry, Blue-eyed Betty, Blond Barbara, Big Ears Ed, Slim Jim, Hairy Barry, and so on.

FAQ

When I'm at parties, I frequently see people whom I have met before, but I can't remember their names. What can I do to avoid being put into the extremely embarrassing position of having to say, "I've forgotten your name"?

Sometimes, no matter what you do, you simply can't come up with the person's name. Here are a few additional "guerrilla" strategies for finding out people's names:

- Ask the host or someone else to identify the guests for you.
- As you are engaged in conversations, carefully listen as

other guests use names. Make quick associations right away.

- If possible, peek at a guest list or seating arrangement. Seeing names in print may help you figure out who's who.

Another surefire method is to reintroduce yourself with, "Hello, do you remember me? I'm Don. We met quite a while ago at . . ." In most cases, the other person will be thankful that you volunteered your name and will do likewise. If he or she doesn't, you can simply ask, "And your name again is . . . ?"

And if all else fails, you can say with a sheepish grin, "Of course I know your name, but my mind has just gone blank."

With Practice, You Can Become Really Good at Remembering Names

You may think it takes a long time to learn how to form associations with the people you meet. The opposite is usually true, and with practice and confidence, making associations becomes instantaneous. If you perform these mental operations all the time, your ability to learn and recall first names will improve tremendously. Then, when you see people you've met before and you use their names, they'll say, "I can't believe you remembered my name!"

Remembering Someone's Name Has a Lasting Effect

The rapport that comes from remembering someone's name makes people instantly like you. As a result, a good conversation will probably begin spontaneously, and you'll both feel good about talking to each other. But something else may happen, too. Just remembering his or her name could be the start of a new friendship!

Part II

Continuing Your Conversations with Wit and Charm

4

Keeping the Conversation Going Strong

Form a concrete concept of what you want by verbalizing your dream and you become more eloquent in describing it.

—Les Brown, author and motivational speaker

Once you've broken the ice by saying hello and making a comment or asking a few questions, do you get "tongue-tied"?

Sustaining conversations is easy if you know the key factors involved. Of course, good body language, displaying interest and curiosity, and being friendly and enthusiastic are essential. Here are six additional keys to sustaining conversations easily and naturally.

1. Focus on the situation you are in.
2. Find out about the "big" events in the other person's life.
3. Balance the two-way information exchange.
4. Discuss topics that are important to you.
5. Change topics using free information.
6. Seek out common interests and experiences.

Keeping the Conversation Going

Key Words
People, places, things, and other specific details that "paint pictures" for the listener.

Free Information
Facts and details a speaker volunteers without specifically being asked.

Instructions
Step-by-step procedures to accomplish a task or objective.

Iceberg Statements
Information, feelings, or interests conveyed indirectly through implied statements or objects.

Hot Buttons
Enthusiastic topics of conversation or strong personal interests.

Common Interests
Areas of mutual experience and involvement.

Key No. 1: Focus on the Situation You Are In

Begin by identifying yourself in your immediate environment, that is, right in the room or place where you happen to be. Why are you here? Who else is here that you already know or want to meet? What activities take place here? How did you come to be in this place? What makes this place unusual or interesting? What can you find out about this place from someone else? What previous experiences have you had in this place? How do you feel about this place?

You can converse with others simply by focusing on the various aspects of your immediate surroundings. Once you identify yourself, it's natural to find out what others are doing in this place. This approach can provide many conversational topics. You don't have to think of *what* to say. Just observe your situation and find something to ask or comment about.

Look Outward—Not Inward

Many poor conversationalists tend to look and think inward rather than focusing on surrounding people and events. They think about how they look, what others might think about them, and whether they are liked. They wonder if people will think they are intelligent or stupid, attractive or ugly, and so on. These "inward" thoughts will make you feel self-conscious and almost totally unaware of what is occurring around you. As a result, all that conversational fuel right in front of your eyes, ears, and nose is lost. Instead, use your senses to pick up the details around you and use them in conversation. In addition, when you think and look outward, you'll be less self-conscious and uncomfortable. Your self-confidence will increase, fear and self-doubt will diminish, and your conversations will become more natural and sustained.

Think of Your Situation as a Series of Concentric Circles

If you focus your conversation on your immediate surroundings, it's easy to expand your topics to the next immediate environment. For example, if you're in an adult education class, then the classroom is your immediate environment, or the center of the concentric circles. After you discuss the class, broaden the conversation to the next circle out to include the school or neighborhood. Focus on the various elements of your surroundings—other classes, the campus, restaurants in the area, movie theaters, clubs, etc. As you continue, broaden your discussion to include where you live, how you travel to class, recreational areas nearby, the city, or interesting outlying areas. Once you realize the enormous amount of conversational fuel directly available, you'll never be at a loss for words.

For example, suppose this is your first time at the health club, and you've finally signed up for that exercise class you've been promising yourself for months. An attractive person is next to you in line waiting to register. Finding out what the other person hopes to gain from the class is a good beginning. After making eye contact and smiling, say hello and ask a question or make a comment based on your immediate situation. Be sure to volunteer your own goals too. The conversation might go something like this:

Roberto: Hi! Are you signing up for the beginning racketball class?

Mary: I sure am! I've been waiting to learn how to play this game right for a long time—and now I'm finally going to do it. What about you?

Roberto: Me, too! I've always been curious about this health club. I drive by it every day on my way to work, so I thought I'd give it a try. Have you taken classes here before?

Mary: I took a swimming course here last summer, and I really enjoyed it. The instructors were excellent, and I met a lot of nice people—plus I learned how to swim!

Roberto: I'm glad you're giving the place a good report. I'm looking forward to this racketball class. By the way, my name's Roberto.

Mary: How do you do. I'm Mary. Have you played racketball before?

Roberto: Not really, I've played a bit of tennis, and a little squash. I like racket games, so I figured it would be fun to learn racketball. Besides, I want to find a regular playing partner, and I thought that this would be a good way to find one. What brings you to the racketball class?

Mary: A friend told me it's pretty easy to learn and great exercise. Plus I really want to meet new people, so here I am! I think the class is going to be a lot of fun.

Roberto: I'm curious, Mary. Do you know if the food in the club lounge is any good? I'm always starved after a good workout.

Mary: I've heard it's pretty good, but I've never tried it.

Roberto: Well, if you're interested, maybe we could meet for a bite to eat or a cold drink after class?

Mary: Sure! That sounds like a great idea! I'll meet you in front of the lounge.

Roberto: All right! See you after class!

In Roberto's conversation with Mary, they discussed reasons for taking the class, previous experience with racket games, the staff at the club, the food in the lounge, and finally a planned meeting for later. Based on the free information disclosed during the conversation, here are some more questions or comments that could have sustained the conversation for a much longer period of time:

> What do you think of the club facilities?
> Have you been taking classes here for a long time?
> What other activities do they have here?
> Do you live in the area?
> Where do you work?
> Do you know where there are some good restaurants in the area?
> Do you have other racketball partners?
> What kind of work do you do?
> What do you do on your days off?
> Would you like to meet for a game sometime?

Key No. 2: Find Out About the Big Events in the Person's Life

Hot Buttons

Dale Carnegie in *How To Win Friends and Influence People* said if you find the really big events in a person's life, conversation won't be a problem. "Hot buttons" are areas that are of keen interest to and create enthusiasm in people you talk with and in yourself. These are subjects that you or your conversational partner can really "get into" and talk about for an extended period of time. Hot buttons can be work, a new job, a hobby, a career goal, an upcoming trip, a sporting activity, a personal dedication to a social cause, and even sex! Hot buttons are subjects or activities that really interest people. A hot button can be a lifelong interest, a passing fancy, or a current fascination—whatever turns you on!

It's important to find other people's hot buttons as soon as possible because these strong interests are extremely fertile areas for sustained conversations. The sooner you find the other person's hot buttons and reveal your own, the more energetic and stimulating conversations you'll have—and you might discover that you share some strong personal interests.

One goal of asking ritual questions is to discover the other person's hot buttons. When you know someone's hot button, you know how to "turn him on" and you also find out what he considers important. You discover where he puts his time, money, and effort—that is, what he values. This is bountiful fuel for conversation, and it tells you insightful things about the person you're speaking with.

In addition to finding out what turns a person on, search for common goals, experiences, and ideas. People often have many topics they're interested in and willing to talk about. Since we all share common interests, it's important to fish for hot buttons in others. When you find someone with hot buttons similar to yours, you'll be able to find out if he would like to share those activities and interests with you. This is where friendships begin to develop.

How to Find Someone Else's Hot Buttons

When you walk into a room full of strangers, do you say to yourself: "I don't have anything in common with the people here!"? Many people think their interests are unique and that others wouldn't be interested. The opposite is usually true. Because of our accessibility to a wide range of activities, many people share common interests, goals, and life experiences.

"Hot Buttons" Are High-Interest Topics

The trick is to find out about others, and discover which ones you have in common.

When seeking someone's hot buttons, fish around subject areas with ritual questions. When you receive an enthusiastic response, express interest in the subject. This doesn't mean you must have a strong interest, but it helps if you can generate a medium or slight curiosity in the subject. This allows the other person an opportunity to share some important aspects of her life with you and will create positive feelings toward you. Your partner will feel that you care about her, and, hopefully, she will express a similar interest in you.

Often people wear or carry items that are hot button indicators. Look for sporting equipment, books, jewelry, clothing, or anything that might provide a clue to the person's hot button. People participate in activities that are hot buttons. Focus on these activities by asking open-ended ritual questions, and sustaining conversations will be easy. Look for people having fun and striving for self-improvement or personal gain, and you'll be closer to finding a person's hot button.

Often people reveal their hot buttons through iceberg statements—that is, they make a statement that reveals the tip of the conversational iceberg, and they're just waiting to be asked the particulars of an activity or project they are involved in. Listen carefully for free information and ask open-ended follow-up questions to encourage people to talk about what they're into. You can say: "That's something I've always been curious about. How did you get involved?"

If there are few visual or verbal clues to a person's hot button, then signal your desire to learn more about what is important to the other person by asking questions such as:

What do you like to do on your days off?
What do you like to do for fun?
What do you like to do when you're not working?
What kinds of things are you interested in?
What do you do to relax?
How do you enjoy spending your free time?

Do you have any projects that you are involved in?

What kinds of hobbies do you enjoy?

Are you involved in any particular organizations?

Have you started any new projects lately?

Is there something that you've always wanted to do, but never got around to it?

Do you have any particular long-term goals?

How You Can Reveal Your Hot Buttons to Others

It's not enough to find the other person's hot buttons. Remember, a good conversation is balanced, so be ready to reveal your hot buttons, too. By letting others know what's important to you, you are giving them an opportunity to get to know you *on your terms* and in a way that makes a good impression.

When you are invited to a party or social event, it is helpful to write down a half dozen or so topics that you're excited about and are willing to share with those you meet. Take this personal inventory of your hot buttons—projects, future plans, or world events—and talk about them enthusiastically with those around you.

Share Your Hot Buttons

When you share your hot buttons, be as specific as possible about your involvement. Use plenty of facts, examples, dates, and places so your conversational partner has lots of free information to question you about. Your partner may not know much about the topic, but your enthusiasm will be contagious and will provide plenty of fuel for your partner to ask follow-up questions.

Here are some ways to tell others about your hot buttons:

I'm really excited about . . .

Guess what, I'm finally going to . . .
I sure am looking forward to this weekend because . . .
I just finished working on . . .
I'm getting ready to begin a big project involving . . .

Take care not to use jargon or technical terms when discussing topics with people who aren't familiar with your hot button. Give them an inside look at what excites you about the topic, rather than overly specific details. Avoid talking about your own hot buttons too much; it's a common pitfall. Be sensitive to how much time you devote to your hot button without hearing again from the other person. It's all right to let someone know what turns you on, but be aware that the other person may not necessarily want to hear everything you have to say about that topic. If you get go-ahead signals (like several follow-up questions), then continue with a few more sentences until you sense that the conversation should return to the other person.

Seek Common Interests

Many people are pleasantly surprised to find that people they meet share common interests. Through active conversation, you get closer to particular goals associated with that subject. Of course, the more interests you have and are able to discuss, the more fulfilling your conversations will be.

Remember that conversation is a way to learn about many things that you have not experienced directly, like traveling to far-off places or skydiving. When you and your conversational partner share experiences, both of you will profit from the exchange. So keep Dale Carnegie's advice in mind: find out the really big things in people's lives and encourage them to talk about them. Seek someone else's hot button, and be sure to reveal your own, too, and keeping the conversation going will be easy.

Key No. 3: Balance the Two-Way Information Exchange

In a good conversation, the participants are aware of the two-way information exchange passing between them. This information exchange should be a balance between talking and listening. Good conversation is like playing a game of catch. First one person has the conversational ball and talks, and then after a bit tosses the conversation to the other person. This "toss" can be in the form of a question, a request for an opinion, or a comment from the person whose turn it is to talk. Once your partner picks up the conversational ball, he can carry the topic further or change topics. By tossing the conversational ball back and forth, the participants can balance the sending and receiving of information about one another.

Good Conversation Is a Balance of Talking and Listening

For a conversation to be stimulating and sustained, the participants must be active talkers as well as active listeners. Be sure to do both in conversation. Make a point of throwing the conversational ball to the other person after you have presented your ideas in an abridged form. Some people feel they have to give long-winded explanations of their views. This is usually unnecessary, confusing, and even boring to your partner. It's better to paint the big picture first, and if your partner wants to know more, you can always fill in with details. Keep your comments and questions focused on big ideas rather than extraneous details, and you'll keep to the point. This way you won't confuse or bore your listener.

Balance the Information You Exchange

While people speak, they should be exchanging basic personal information, ideas, opinions, facts, and details at about the same rate. This doesn't mean a tit-for-tat exchange, but rather a general balance within the context of the conversation. When the exchange of information is balanced, you can get to know one another at the same rate—little bits at a time. If your conversation is active, a lot of information will pass between you, and in the end each participant will have learned quite a bit about the other.

This is a natural way of getting to know people, and it will promote trust while encouraging both parties to disclose more personal information. "Good listeners" may feel that they don't need to disclose information about themselves, and that their disclosures are dull and boring. They might think: "Who cares where I'm from, or what I do, or where I went to school?! I'll bore the person to death!" It's important to be a good listener, but being an equal participant is also very necessary and important.

If one participant discloses too much and the other discloses too little, then the conversation is unbalanced. An unbalanced conversation will make both parties uncomfortable. One might think: "I did all the talking. She just sat there like a bump on a log!" In contrast, the other person will be thinking: "He never shut up! It was nonstop gab—I almost passed out!"

It's easy to understand why an unbalanced conversation results in a negative impression. If the information flow is balanced, including ritual information, small talk, and more personal self-disclosures, then the participants will feel they have gotten to know each other in a natural and nonthreatening way. The more balanced your exchanges are, the more quickly you'll really get to know the person and the more likely the relationship will flourish.

Key No. 4: Discuss Topics That Are Important to You

It's essential to let others know what you consider important and meaningful. The best way to reveal your values and attitudes to others is to discuss topics of concern and interest to you. These could be religion, politics, or current events, but whatever the topic, take the initiative and disclose some of your feelings and values.

When you talk about events that are important to you, the other person gets an idea of your personality, and it also provides an enormous well of conversational material.

What makes you tick? Why do you feel the way that you do about things? What are your concerns? What is your vision for the future? What are your likes and preferences? The answers to these questions tell others how you relate to the world around you.

Small talk is not just meaningless and shallow. Recognize that ritual questions and self-disclosure provide an environment for revealing more personal thoughts and feelings and also give more credibility and consistency to your views.

While expressing your ideas, you may hear yourself say things you have never said before. For many, conversation is when their ideas are formulated and developed into orderly concepts for the first time. When you discuss different ideas, it's important to do it in such a way that the other participant knows he is entitled to his opinion, too—even it if differs from yours. Be receptive to your partner's point of view and listen carefully to what he has to say. When it's your turn to give your opinion, your partner will be more receptive and open to your ideas.

A few words of caution: when telling someone what's important to you, be careful not to spill your guts, tell all, or get on a soapbox. Don't complain mercilessly about things you or your listeners can't do anything about. Leave very personal information out of your conversation, especially in the early stages. There is a time to tell friends things about yourself that are more personal. Wait until the time is right, and you've established trust. By disclosing what's important in a natural way you will let others in on what's important in your life.

Key No. 5: Change Topics Using Free Information

Changing topics is probably the easiest way to sustain a conversation while fishing for mutual interest areas with your partner. You don't have to talk out one topic before proceeding to the next. Good conversations are normally an interweaving of subjects and ideas, and it's not uncommon for participants to jump from point to point. It's helpful to stay within generally related subject areas, but if your discussion proceeds into new areas, you can always return to the original topic by saying, "Getting back to what you said before about . . ."

FAQ

I'm lunching with a client, and I don't want to talk about business since our morning and afternoon are concerned with business. How do I make interesting informal conversation during lunch?

When you are with a client, it is important to know something about her outside interests. In many cases, if you have met before, you can obtain this information through free information. If this is your first contact, then doing your homework prior to a planned meeting can make a big difference when it comes to casual conversation. Without prying, find out what your client's personal interests are. When you sit down to lunch, simply say, "I understand you are quite a flower gardener. How long have you been involved in that?" or "I understand that you are a volunteer for . . . I'd love to hear about what you're doing for that organization."

If you don't have any inside information about the person, be particularly attentive for free information. Perhaps the person will mention in passing about being in Hawaii for a business conference. You can say, "I heard you mention earlier that you were in Hawaii. Did you enjoy your stay in the islands?" or "Had you been there before?"

Be sure to reveal enough free information about yourself throughout the conversation so that he will know what follow-up questions to ask you. When you sense a certain topic has been talked out, then change the subject by referring to some free information revealed earlier, or offer some new information of your own. Say: "It's interesting to hear you talk about sailing, because I like it as well. In fact, I just got back from a two-week trip off the coast of California, and it was great!"

Here are some other conversation starters you can use while dining with a client:

How did you happen to wind up in this line of work?
What did you do before you joined your company?
Have you ever wanted to own your own business?
What new trends do you see coming in our industry?
What do you think of . . . ? (Refer to an interesting news or industry event.)
Have you seen any good movies lately?
I just read a terrific book about . . . Do you like to read?
You obviously pay attention to your diet. What else do you do to stay in such good shape?
Do you have any special vacation plans coming up?
Are you interested in food as much as I am?

Refer to Free Information—"I Heard You Mention Earlier . . ."

The most common method of changing topics is to refer to previously revealed free information by commenting or asking a closed-ended ritual question. For example, "I remember you mentioned earlier that you were in Hawaii last month. Were you there for business or pleasure?" Always listen carefully and remember free information since it can provide good conversational fuel. If the topic you've been discussing has run its course, just change the topic by inserting an open-ended ritual question based on your own or your partner's free information.

Sometimes you might want to change to another topic for only a brief moment. All you have to do is say: "Excuse me, but I'd like to change the subject for a moment," and then make your comment or ask your question. Try to complete your ideas quickly and then return to your original topic of discussion.

Be careful to maintain focus. Jumping from topic to topic can give your partner the impression that you cannot (or don't care to) discuss an issue on a meaningful level. It may also indicate that you are not listening or that you are bored with the subject matter—both of which may be true! If your partner gives you a brief response, she may not wish to discuss the topic for a particular reason. Be sensitive to unenthusiastic responses, and be ready to change to a new topic quickly when you feel you have touched on a high-sensitivity or low-interest area for the other person.

Let's Change the Subject!

What do you do if someone brings up a negative or inappropriate subject—especially at a party or social event? These are subjects that are in poor taste, "downers," or generally unhappy topics that make people uncomfortable. For example, if someone makes a racial slur in an attempt to be funny, to attract attention, or to get a conversation going, you can show that you don't have the same opinion. Do so without a lot of emotional discussion. Simply say: "I don't really agree with that," or "I'm sure we can find more pleasant things to talk about," or "I'll forgive you for asking that question, if you'll forgive me for not answering it."

You've made the suggestion to change the subject, so it's up to you to do just that. Pick up the conversational ball quickly and open a new topic of discussion by making a comment or asking an open-ended question based on free information that you heard earlier before the conversation took an unfortunate turn. Usually the other participants will feel relieved that the negative topic didn't last too long.

Use Key Words to Change Topics

Listen for Key Words, Facts, and Details—and Remember Them!

Listen carefully for words, facts, and details, and refer to them as your conversation continues. This shows that you are listening and interested in what is being said, and also serves as conversational fuel. You can control the conversation's direction simply by focusing your comments and questions on these facts and details.

Your conversations will progress along a pathway of exchange. Once you discover mutual interest areas, you can continually return to and explore them as new ideas come to mind.

Key No. 6: Seek Out Common Interests and Experiences

Suppose you meet a person and you really hit it off. Usually you'll think: "I really like this person. We have a lot in common. I can relate to his feelings and emotions. We have fun together. We get along well. I can be myself. He listens to me and understands what I'm talking about."

It's important to let your conversational partner know when you can identify with him. When you can relate to something directly or indirectly, respond in a way that lets your partner know you are listening and understanding and can personally identify with it. For example, if you are discussing someone's recent trip to a location where you have visited, lived, or are preparing to visit, interject a quick comment or question based on your experience about that place, such as: "I used to live there," or "I went to school there," or "What's it like there?" or "I'm due to go out there next month," or "I've always wanted to go there."

Quick inserts will provide your conversational partner with immediate feedback and let him know that you can relate to the subject. Make quick connections and you can direct the flow of the conversation in a natural way. When you couple this with open body language and active listening, you are signaling your partner to continue with a particular topic. In this way, you can identify areas of mutual interest and experiences as they occur in the conversation. When there is a slight lull in the conversation, you can always refer back to an area of mutual interest you heard earlier. If you don't let the other person know that you relate to several details of his conversation, then he might assume you're not interested in discussing them.

When you make connections with your partner's experience, you also give him free information to pick up on. Remember, most people have many interests, and they want to find which interests you have in common. Let your partner know by saying: "Oh, really! I like that too!" or "Me too!" or "Gee, I don't meet many people who are interested in that, too."

When you let the other person know you can identify with a topic, experience, or goal, you create a bridge between you and him. Each bridge that you build gives you the opportunity to return for more conversation. The more bridges you build, the more you will be able to share with one another.

When you meet someone and discover areas of common interest and experience, you gain building blocks to develop a deeper relationship. Remember, much of the point of conversation is to discuss different topics and experiences in order to find a common bond. This gives you and your partner an opportunity to decide if you would like to get to know one another better. If you have enough in common, then hopefully you will want to see each other again to share common interests. So, when you discover a connection, tell your partner right away. This creates a sense of familiarity and indicates your interest in discussing the topic further and sharing your ideas. This is the stuff that friendships are made of.

5

Getting Your Ideas Across

Be sincere; be brief; be seated.
—Franklin D. Roosevelt, (1882–1945), 32nd U.S. president

Several factors can keep the speaker from getting his ideas across to others. People have a *resistance to change* for many different reasons. We are creatures of habit, and we tend to hold on to certain ways of thinking, feeling, and behaving. Our fixed attitudes provide real or imaginary gains, and we feel comfortable and free from the fear of being taken advantage of. Resistance to change is reinforced by the attitude that it's safer *not* to trust people.

Another common problem that complicates reaching others is that sometimes you are competing for their attention. Instead of listening to your every word, the other participant is often thinking her own thoughts and tuning you out. Because of her low listening and attention span, your ideas and arguments become lost or misunderstood. Common signs of wandering attention include your partner asking unnecessary questions, making irrelevant comments, and bringing up arguments that have already been discussed and answered. These factors indicate that the other person is not tuned in to your thinking, and isn't ready to adopt or consider your ideas.

A third factor that interferes with communication with others is *wishful hearing*. What you say is often misunderstood by the listener because he interprets it to mean something he really wants to hear—not what you actually said or intended.

Wishful hearing can take the form of jumping to conclusions based on a few isolated facts or actions, and it results in giving meaning that originates only in the listener's mind.

A fourth reason why you may not get your ideas through to others is that you make *unwarranted assumptions* about the other person. You may assume that others know and understand many things that you take for granted. Unwarranted assumptions are reinforced when your partner remains silent and mechanically nods his head, implying acceptance or understanding and encouraging you to continue thinking that he is right with you.

When it finally appears that the listener doesn't have a clue about what you have been saying, the situation can become rather awkward. You will feel that you have been talking to yourself, and the listener will feel like an idiot.

Finally, people who maintain a veil of *habitual secrecy* about what they think and feel tend to be resentful when you ask them what they do or any other common ritual question. These people experience your curiosity as a threat to their security, and as a result, they tend to act defensive and unfriendly.

All of us have secrets, even from those we know and trust a great deal. This is natural. The degree to which a person keeps her thoughts secret determines her receptivity to outside influences and persuasion. Getting your ideas through to people who won't tell you what their ideas are is difficult. Such people have a low receptivity level and aren't likely to accept your ideas.

FAQ

It's so hard to get my co-workers to even consider my ideas! How can I get them to be more open to what I have to say?

Opening Channels

Encouraging Cooperation and Receptivity

There are ways to overcome difficulties in presenting your ideas to others. Begin to encourage cooperation and receptivity by *telling others the purpose of your conversation.* "The reason I'm calling is . . ." or "I'm new in the neighborhood. Do you happen to know a good restaurant nearby?" or "I've always wanted to be able to do that! Will you show me how?" or "I'm going to be traveling there soon. Do you know . . ." or "I'd like to talk to you about . . ." These types of self-disclosures create a sense of trust in you and will allow your partner to feel more comfortable in responding. If you don't gain your partner's trust, most likely she won't share opinions or feelings with you.

When you ask a question, tell the person why you want to know. If you don't reveal the purpose of your questions, the other person might feel nervous, suspicious, or uncomfortable. She may think you don't believe her and are trying to find out if she is really telling the truth. Tell your motivation for asking the question, and your partner will be more inclined to answer without being overly cautious.

Another essential factor in gaining people's cooperation and receptivity is *developing respect for others.* Many of our attitudes and feelings are communicated without words, and how we listen to other people's ideas tells them how we think and feel about them. When you show that you care, a person will more likely confide in and trust you. When you ask for someone's opinions, you're actually giving a compliment because you are saying that you value that person's viewpoint.

Don't ignore people's feelings, and you'll be encouraging cooperation and receptivity for you to present your ideas.

A good way to increase your sensitivity while talking to others is to ask yourself questions like:

How will what I'm saying make the other person feel?
How will he react to what I'm saying?
Will he feel complimented or put down by what I'm saying?

By *taking the other person's viewpoint,* you will be projecting your own receptivity and, as a result, will lower her defenses and open the channels of communication. It also makes you more aware of implied or hidden meanings accompanying conversation.

Explore Irrelevant Comments

When you hear ideas that seem irrelevant, explore their purpose. Don't insist that all comments be relevant by ignoring or dismissing comments that seem extraneous or off the subject. *Accepting the other person's sense of relevancy* will broaden the conversation to include his purpose as well as yours. This encourages your partner to cooperate with you because you're showing that you see things from his point of view. As a result, he'll be open to your ideas. Cooperation and receptivity increase when you show your partner that you consider his ideas as important and valid as your own.

6

Overcoming Conversational Hang-ups

The only way to get the best of an argument is to avoid it.
—Dale Carnegie (1888–1955), author of
How to Win Friends and Influence People

Many conversational problems are the result of misconceptions or negative attitudes toward those you wish to communicate with and/or yourself.

Most conversational hang-ups are rooted in fear. Frequently, they relate to how other people will judge you. These hang-ups tend to prevent you from reaching out to others in an honest and sincere way and they can be considered conversation blocks.

The most common conversational hang-ups and some ways of rationalizing them are:

1. *"I'm right—you're wrong!" (Arguing)*
   Always be right. Never lose an argument. Show others that your opinion is better.
2. *"I can read a person like a book." (Stereotyping)*
   Draw quick conclusions about those you meet based on isolated statements or actions.
3. *"It doesn't matter to me." (Being nonassertive)*

Always go out of your way to please others, and they will like and respect you. Stay out of the decision-making process to show that you are a flexible person. Don't do your own thing, because people may disapprove, or become offended or upset.

4. *"Tell me something I don't know." (Bragging)*
Being a know-it-all will impress the people you talk with.

5. *"I'm boring." (Copping out)*
Don't talk, because you don't have anything really interesting to say.

Hang-up No.1—"I'm Right—You're Wrong!"

Some people think that good conversation means winning an argument or discussion. They present their opinions as indisputable facts. This type of conversationalist will go out of his way to show that his opinions are better than those of the people he's talking with. His goal is to never lose an argument, show that he is right, and "win" the conversation.

It's common for competitive conversationalists to put down other people's opinions by making comments like "That's the most ridiculous thing I've ever heard!" or "I think what you are saying is utter nonsense!" This attitude sends a clear message to the person you're talking with: "Since we differ in opinion, and I'm right—you are therefore wrong." There's another message that accompanies this communication: "Since I'm right, I'm better and smarter than you."

Needless to say, this closed and aggressive attitude will not allow others to open up to you in any real, meaningful way—

especially in the more emotionally sensitive areas. Manipulative put-downs make people feel foolish and stupid and, as a result, tend to lower their level of self-esteem. This doesn't make them feel comfortable with you or allow them to feel as though they can trust you with more self-disclosures.

The misconception here is that people who feel they always have to be right or have to win a discussion think that others will respect their opinions more if they are rigidly committed to their view. As a result of this nonreceptive position, they send this signal to those they talk with: "Anyone who disagrees with me is obviously wrong, and therefore a fool!"

It's easy to see why *"I'm right—you're wrong"* can ruin a conversation and throw cold water on a developing friendship or relationship.

Don't Assume That Everything You Know or Believe Is Absolutely True

When discussing topics from differing points of view, remember there's a major difference between absolute fact and what we assume to be true. Often, our opinions are the result of preferences, biases, assumptions, and our conditioning—not necessarily facts. As a result, there are many gray areas where differences of opinions can be discussed at great length with others. These areas are very fertile ground for good conversation.

Every person has the right to his point of view—even if it seems strange or totally absurd to you—without being put down or ridiculed. Don't force your views upon others. Show a desire to understand your partner's point of view. Thus, you will encourage him to open up to you more and be more receptive to your ideas. This is especially important when you are trying to get your ideas and feelings across.

How to Say "I Don't Agree with You"

When someone says something you disagree with, avoid conversation killers like "You're dead wrong!" or "Where in heaven's name did you ever pick up such a stupid idea?" When you voice a difference of opinion, preface your statement with "It seems to me . . ." "Here's the way I see it . . ." "I think . . ." "I believe . . ." "It's my impression . . ." "In my opinion . . ." "I feel differently about it . . ." or "It's been my experience . . ." When you present opinions this way, without condemning the other person's statement, she will be more likely to listen to what you are about to say, rather than putting up a defensive barrier to your ideas.

If someone disagrees with what you have said or believe, don't say, "You tasteless slob! Don't you know who you're talking to?" It's better to say, "I guess we just regard this differently," or "I can see that you disagree. You're entitled to your own opinion," or "Well, different strokes for different folks!" If you don't like something and want to communicate this without offending the other person, say: "Well, that may be a great piece of music (art, movie, play, etc.), but I didn't particularly care for it." Remember, you're entitled to your opinion, and so are the people you talk with. Be sure to send this signal clearly and the "I'm right—you're wrong" hang-up won't ruin your conversations.

Hang-up No. 2— "I Can Read a Person Like a Book!"

People who make this statement often form hasty conclusions from a person's individual comments or actions. When you jump to conclusions about someone, you may be unconsciously reacting to the person's stereotype. If your partner fulfills one characteristic of a stereotype, then that's all it takes to elicit this negative approach of "sizing her up."

Can You Tell a Book by Its Cover?

People who jump to conclusions about others based on single experiences are just as likely to believe that you can tell a great deal about a person by the automobile he drives, his occupation, and his clothing. Of course, you can learn about others from these details, but if you rely heavily on these, your conclusions are more likely based on previous experiences or preconceived notions. As a result, this method of learning about people evokes stereotypical images—not individual qualities. People don't like being stereotyped, and they sense when it occurs. In response, they may stereotype you, and the communication channel closes.

Separate Specific Isolated Behavior From Total Personality

Reserve judgment about people until you have enough data to form a more accurate conclusion about what they are really like. Give the people an opportunity to get to know you in a real and meaningful way. Extend an open attitude toward others, and most likely the same attitude will be returned. If you are the victim of a put-down or a stereotypical remark that is not an accurate reflection of you, such as, "Boy, are you ever a scatterbrained person!" be sure to clarify that while you may sometimes seem a little scatterbrained, you are usually a pretty down-to-earth person.

Hang-up No. 3—"It Doesn't Matter to Me"

Some people believe that if they place other people's needs before their own, they will be liked and respected, and in addition, that people will return the favor sometime. People are often disappointed when this unrealistic expectation is unfulfilled. Some think that they are being taken advantage of and they become resentful.

People who say "It doesn't matter to me" are doing two different things. First, they are attempting to please others by seeking approval for their behavior. If they do what the other person wants, then what is there to disapprove of? Second, they are being passive and not taking any responsibility for the decision-making process that accompanies most activities.

It's Good to Be Flexible—but Not Indifferent

You might think that if you are amiable enough to do almost anything someone else wants (even if you'd rather not), this will make you an easy-to-get-along-with person. However, the other person might feel that your "It doesn't matter to me" attitude displays noninvolvement, indifference, boredom, or even insincerity.

Express Your Preferences (Even If They Might Be Contrary to Your Partner's)

If you don't express preferences, tastes, wants, and desires, people won't know what you like or what you are seeking. People are not mind readers, and unless you tell or show them what you want, they just won't know. If you don't express your true feelings, hostility, resentment, and guilt may result.

Assertiveness Pays Off

Assertiveness can be defined as saying directly what you want while respecting the rights and feelings of others. You have the right to do what you want and not to do what you don't want to do. You're entitled to feel as you do, and you don't have to offer reasons or excuses for your feelings or behavior.

Get What You Want by Asking for It

It's better to express what you want by asking for it instead of waiting for someone to guess what you want. Let someone know what you want, and he'll be in a better position to give it to you—or say no. At least you'll have the satisfaction of expressing yourself in an honest and direct manner even if you don't get what you want.

You Have the Right to Say No and Not Feel Guilty About It

If you don't want something, simply say no. People who have trouble saying no are usually afraid of offending or hurting the other person's feelings. If you say yes when you really want to say no, or you're not sure, say: "Let me think about it," or "I'll let you know," or "Let me call you back."

Get Involved—Offer an Alternative

If you say "It doesn't matter to me," you're not involving yourself in the decision-making process that accompanies human interactions. Instead of agreeing to all suggestions that come your way (even if you don't want to), offer some alternatives.

Present your ideas and preferences, and your partner will gain a better sense of who you are, what you want, and your interest in the subject or activity. Become involved in the decision-making process. Don't passively accept anything, and others will know that you care. Involvement translates into interest, enthusiasm, and a desire to be with the other person.

FAQ

Won't people think I'm selfish if I do what I want instead of doing what they want?

Some people feel guilty about doing their own thing and feel that others may disapprove. They believe that people will find them selfish or that they will become offended or hurt.

If you do something that someone doesn't like, being afraid that she'll dislike you prevents you from pursuing your goals and needs. If you live your life in this way, you're overly sensitive to others' approval and what they think of you.

"But What Will People Think of Me?"

It's important to be sensitive to other people's feelings, but if someone does get upset because of your decisions, then the problem may stem from how he interprets your actions. By asserting your right to act in your own interest, your self-esteem will be much higher than if you simply forgo your wants, needs, and goals because someone doesn't approve. You're destined to a life of frustration and disappointment if you only respond to the world around you based on "What will people think of me?"

Do Your Own Thing

Stand up for your rights and do what you want. Do this assertively by telling others in direct and honest statements what your goals, intentions, and motivations are—*without feeling the need for their approval.*

When you think about what's important for you, try to look ahead a month or two—even further, if possible—and project where you'll be as a result of your actions. Conceptualizing the future is often a key factor in making your pursuits realities instead of just unfulfilled dreams. Be assertive and you can acquire the satisfaction of knowing that you are giving your goals a good try, even if you don't succeed right away.

Caution: Assertiveness Is Not a Justification for Selfishness and Insensitivity

You may think that doing your own thing is an excuse or justification for being insensitive or uncaring about others. Friendships and relationships revolve around giving and receiving. Both are required, and a fair and equitable balance between the two is essential. Assertiveness allows you to take your needs into consideration, but don't discount the effect you have on those around you.

Hang-up No. 4—"Tell Me Something I Don't Know"

Some people feel the need to project the image that they know everything and are good at everything. They are afraid they'll be considered incompetent and stupid if they say, "I don't know."

Being a "know-it-all" can effectively kill conversations because you convey the message that the other person's ideas and feelings don't matter to you. This cuts off the two-way exchange of information, ideas, and feelings, and only serves to elevate you to a superior position at the other's expense. Considering the fact that we all have major limitations in our expertise and experience, this is a rather unrealistic and doubtful image to project to others. It becomes increasingly clear that you're just trying to boost your ego without honestly communicating.

It's Okay to Say "I Don't Know"

Saying "I don't know" is likely to make your partner respect you for your honesty rather than put you down for your ignorance. It's counterproductive for conversation to think that you (or anybody else) are required to know answers to every question or be aware of everything and everybody.

Suppose someone mentions a book, movie, or famous person in a discussion, and you nod your head knowingly as though you know exactly what he's talking about. It may come out later (as many times it does) that you didn't really have the direct experience you projected, and your partner will get the impression that you were just faking the conversation. This inhibits the conversation and your partner will generally form a negative impression and tend to distrust your future statements.

"I'm Not Familiar with That . . . Fill Me In!"

To avoid projecting a false image, admit your shortcomings, lack of experience, or ignorance about a certain subject, and look for your partner's response. In most cases (unless the other person is trying to put you down), your partner will accept what you know and don't know. It presents a balanced picture of you and tends to create a more trustworthy personal image.

Hang-up No. 5—"I'm Boring"

Some people take the easy way out and don't participate in conversations. They think that they have nothing interesting to say. This is a cop-out and self-imposed put-down. Copping out is a way to avoid facing people, situations, and problems. Those who are afraid of boring others or say they don't want to make the effort required to carry on a conversation are really not giving themselves a chance.

Give Yourself a Break

You're being too hard on yourself if your inner voice keeps saying, "No one is interested in what I have to say." Of course, you know that people can't read your mind, but often they will interpret your silence as boredom, lack of interest, or a desire to end the conversation. This will likely leave them with a poor impression of you and make them want to go talk to someone else.

Focus on the Positive Events in Your Life—and Talk about Them

Focus on the positive events in your life—events or experiences that you're excited about—and your enthusiasm will project to others. It's beneficial to talk about things that are important to you, and to express your ideas, opinions, and feelings. It tells others who you are and what's important to you, and it helps you understand yourself better. Don't cop out, and you won't be boring.

Don't Cop Out

Be aware of these common cop-out statements:

"I don't feel like it." (An excuse for not doing what you want or have to do.)

"I didn't have time." (Another excuse for not doing what you want or have to do.)

"What difference does it make?" (A rationalization for not putting out the effort required to make something happen.)

"I hate it when people ask me what I've been up to." (An avoidance response to someone showing interest in you.)

These hang-ups and cop-outs block the way to meaningful conversations, and they prevent people from developing friendships and relationships. Usually, these attitudes are a matter of habit rather than deep psychological problems, and they can be overcome by changing your thinking and your approach to the people you interact with. Once you break the pattern of these hang-ups, you'll find a difference in how people relate to you. Others will notice a positive change in how you feel about yourself and about them. Your communication channels will be open and accessible to others and this will promote better conversations.

Part III

Ending Your Conversations with a Great Impression

7

Closing Conversations Tactfully

> The real art of conversation is not only to say the right thing in the right place but to leave unsaid the wrong thing at the tempting moment.
> —Lady Dorothy Nevill (1825–1913), British author

All conversations must come to an end sometime. Since there's a natural flow to most conversations, there is a right time to bring conversations to a successful close.

The Best Time to End a Conversation

Whether you are engaged in a brief or lengthy conversation, be aware of the dynamics involved in ending conversations in a positive manner. If you wait too long, you and your partner will feel the strain and become uncomfortable, anxious, or even bored. The easiest moment to end the conversation has already passed.

If you are anxious, especially during short periods of silence, you may end the conversation earlier than necessary, and in an abrupt manner. This will leave your partner with the impression that you don't feel comfortable about the conversation or your partner.

It's best to end a conversation after both parties have expressed themselves to one another, and when the time seems right or demands that you go your separate ways.

It's important to end conversations in a warm and engaging manner, so that you'll both feel good about the exchange that has occurred.

Closing Conversations to Leave a Positive Impression

There are natural pauses between sentences and topics of discussion, and it's wise to wait for these opportune moments to bring your conversations to a close.

End Your Conversations Tactfully

Step 1: Restate something interesting the other person said.

Step 2: Say you enjoyed the chat.

Step 3: (Optional) Say, "Let's talk again soon."

Step 4: Use the person's name and say goodbye.

When you feel the time is right to close the conversation—that is, the discussion has come to a conclusion, or one of the parties has to leave—take an active role and begin to send signals that you are ready to leave. Briefly summarize the main ideas your partner has been expressing. This shows the other person that you were listening and that you understood, and it also signals a conclusion to the discussion.

If you are discussing a particular current event, and you want to send a conclusion signal, you could say, "It certainly sounds like you're well informed about the problem. I'll read that article you were talking about."

After you send a signal that you want to end a conversation, it's good to plan to see the other person again (only if you really want to) by setting a meeting for the future. Instead of closing with the customary cliché, "Why don't we get together sometime?" (which usually means never), be more specific about an event such as a movie or dinner, and a time within the next week or so.

In a friendly and direct way, you could say: "I've really had a lot of fun talking with you, _____. How about getting together next week for dinner or a movie? I'll give you a call."

In this way, you express your interest in your partner while leaving an open invitation to meet again. This is particularly effective for developing friendships and relationships.

Remember to use your partner's name when you say good-bye, and use open, friendly body language (eye contact, smiling, and a warm handshake). Then be on your way. Avoid long, drawn-out good-byes.

Getting Out of Problem Conversations

There are times when the nature of a conversation, or the person you're speaking with, makes you prefer to end the conversation and withdraw sooner than later, but without offending the other person. For example, if you are cornered by a long-winded bore at a party who has been bragging about his exploits for some time, then try the following strategy to end the conversation.

Wait for a slight pause between words or sentences, and then quickly interject (an acceptable form of interruption) a few rapid yes/no or closed-ended questions, thus interrupting the bore's flow of words and giving you the conversational ball. (Remember, you can direct a conversation by asking questions.) Then restate in a few sentences an acknowledgment of your partner's last few statements, and get ready to make your getaway. You can say: "Well, it sounds like you enjoy your work! Good luck on your next project. I'm going to mosey along and say hello to a friend of mine," or "I'm going to get some hors d'oeuvres now, if you'll excuse me." After smiling, shaking hands, and using his name say, "It was nice talking to you." Then move directly out of the situation.

You may be worrying, "But what if I don't know anyone else at the party! I can't just stand around! He'll see me standing there and become offended!" Try this simple solution: Go refill your glass, get something to eat, or visit the bathroom, and then take a few moments to survey the situation. Look for the most open and receptive group or person in the room. Proceed there directly and engage in conversation. If you're really sharp, you can spot your likely person or group before you deliver your conversation closer.

FAQ _____

I hate it when I'm at a party and get trapped by a complainer. I know I need to be a good listener, but after a while I feel like I'm being used. How can I tactfully end a conversation with someone who complains too much?

Handling the Complainer

The complainer usually talks about personal problems, misfortune, sickness, and other unfortunate events. In most cases, people who focus on unpleasant topics are looking for sympathy. No one enjoys listening to the constant complainer. Therefore, after listening for free information and details of the problem, ask a few yes/no or closed-ended questions to break the flow of complaints and to allow you to direct the conversation to a conclusion.

Express some words of sympathy such as, "It sounds like you're having a tough time," or "I'm sorry to hear that you're having so much trouble." This will indicate to the other person that you have been listening and empathize with her problem.

When handling the complainer, it is perfectly acceptable to offer a few words of unsolicited advice or general words of wisdom and encouragement such as: "Just hang in there— it'll work out," or "If it makes you feel any better, you're not the only one who is having that problem." Then, with sincere feeling, say: "I hope things work out for you," smile, give the person a warm handshake, and say: "I'm going to go say hello to a friend of mine." Then say good-bye, using the person's name, and move quickly out of the situation.

FAQ

My friend always dumps all his problems on me when he calls on the telephone. He moans that his girlfriend isn't around enough, that he's unappreciated on the job, and that his parents still treat him like a child. I know that good friends are supposed to be good listeners, but after a while I feel like I'm being used. How can I tactfully end the conversation?

It's gratifying to help a friend who has troubles, and yes, a good friend is a good listener. But, there's a limit to how much complaining even a good friend can listen to. The key word here is *limit.* Limit how much time you devote to discussing a friend's problems and advice that you offer. No matter how much you might want to help, the truth is that no one can solve your friend's problems, except him.

Limit the time you talk about his problems by first empathizing with his plight. This validates his feelings and shows you are listening. Asking him to come up with some options clearly demonstrates that you're not going to be his problem solver. For example, you might say, "Sam, it sounds like you're going through a rough time at work right now. So what are your options?" He may respond that he doesn't have a clue, with the hope that you will offer advice or continue discussing his problem. Instead, you can say, "Well, I'm sure you can come up with something."

Since friendship is a two-way street, you have the right to expect him to be a good listener, too. Change the subject to something that you want to talk about by saying, "By the way, I've been meaning to tell you about . . ." Then end your conversation on a positive note by saying, "I hope things improve for you at work."

Dealing Assertively with the Manipulator

We've all been in conversations where the person we are speaking with is attempting to make us do something against our wishes. It could be a high-pressured sales pitch or a pushy boss who wants you to work late for the fifth night in a row. In these cases, the goal is to politely end the conversation and not be forced to do something against your wishes.

To the persistent salesperson, say: "I appreciate your enthusiasm, but don't waste any more of your time. I'm not interested. Thank you anyway." When the salesperson doesn't take no for an answer, calmly restate your response, "I'm not interested," over and over again. This effective technique is referred to as the "broken record" and allows you to be persistent without arguing and thus avoid manipulation.

When you are ending a conversation with your boss who always pressures you to work late, it's important to be assertive, but also use common sense. After all, you still want to have a job when you arrive for work the next day. Start by stating assertively what you want, while you let your boss know that you understand and sympathize with the problem. The conversation might go as follows:

Boss: Diane, Jean won't be coming in, so I'm going to need you to stay late tomorrow to finish those reports.

Diane: Gee, Mr. Lund, that's impossible. I have something planned for right after work, and can't miss it.

Boss: Well, you'll just have to change your plans, or be late, because the main office wants those reports in by the next day, or it will be my neck.

Diane: I'd like to be able to help you, Mr. Lund, but I won't be able to work late tomorrow night.

Boss:	You've always been so reliable before, and now you're letting me down. This is really putting me in a tough spot!
Diane:	I understand that you need someone to finish the reports, but I won't be available. This is something I've been planning for a long time.
Boss:	But who am I going to get to finish up those reports?
Diane:	Have you thought about giving Jeff a call? He said he was looking for some extra work. Maybe he can help.
Boss:	Jeff? That's an idea. He might be the solution.
Diane:	Good. I'm sure Jeff would be happy to do the job.
Boss:	Okay Diane, thanks—oh, and have a good time tomorrow night.
Diane:	Thank you, Mr. Lund.

Use Tact and Common Sense When Saying No to Your Boss

Assertive conversations with your supervisor or employer require plenty of tact and common sense. *When* you say no is as important as *how* you say no. Although sometimes you will need to work late, you can tell her that you won't always be available to work overtime. For example, you can say, "I understand that on occasion I'll need to work late. But I have other responsibilities, too, so I won't be available to work past 5:00 P.M. on a regular basis." Hopefully, by putting your boss on notice that your work time is limited, she will make other arrangements when it's necessary.

The Last Few Words

To summarize, when you end conversations:

- Always attempt to end the exchange on a friendly note. This lets the other participant feel good about the exchange.
- Use the other person's name, add a compliment such as: "It's been great talking with you," and then say good-bye with a handshake.
- Attempt to meet the person again for a specific activity at a time not too far into the future—say, a week or so. Say: "I'm looking forward to seeing you again."
- Tell your partner you enjoyed the conversation and you are going to mosey on to chat with someone else, get a drink, say hello to a friend, or whatever you wish to do, and then do it.
- Keep your good-bye short and sweet, and most of all, warm and friendly.

8
Making Friends

If I don't have friends, then I ain't got nothin'.
—Billie Holiday (1915–1959),
jazz singer

The Gift of Friendship

Making friends is a goal if we value companionship. Most people have only a few friends whom they trust completely with their most personal feelings and information. When you give someone your friendship, it becomes an important aspect of a relationship. Unfortunately, there are many who feel they have no one to confide in and call a good friend. This can change, because good friendships can begin at any stage in your life.

What is Friendship?

It has been said that love is blind, and friendship is just not noticing. Friends can be allies, supporters, or sympathizers who give encouragement, feedback, honest opinions, and usually a lot of advice. We reveal things to friends that we just wouldn't say to anyone else. A friend is someone you can trust with sensitive information and know that he won't hold it against you; someone who shares common interests and experiences with you and adds to your sense of fulfillment. Other components of good friendship are:

Patience	Stimulation	Sympathy	Intimacy
Respect	Equality	Fun	Spontaneity
Understanding	Reliability	Flexibility	Another point
Sharing	Helping	Enrichment	of view
Compassion	Learning	Freedom	Tolerance
Trust	Love	Reassurance	Honesty

Making Friends Is Not Always Easy

Making friends takes time, effort, commitment, give-and-take, and a lot of tolerance for the many human frailties we all

Making and Keeping Friends Rests on Four Key Principles

• Take the initiative and reach out to others.

• Show genuine interest in people.

• Treat others with respect and kindness.

• Value yourself and others as unique individuals who have much to offer.

have. Although most people are open to new friendships, life pursuits such as careers and family tend to become a higher priority. Some people feel it takes too much time and effort to develop friendships.

Developing Trust

Another reason why friendships take time to develop is that they require mutual trust between people, and trust takes time to develop. To gain someone's trust, you must reveal some personal information and feelings so that the other person can gain a real sense of what kind of person you are, and what you are sensitive to. As time goes on, you and your friends will disclose more and more personal information, and the trust between you will grow. In the early stages of friendship, people sometimes don't know how much to reveal about themselves. If you are aware of the balance of information being traded back and forth, then your rate of self-disclosure will probably be appropriate.

A firm belief in someone's honesty and reliability can take quite a while to develop, while a breach of trust can destroy a relationship in a very brief period of time. When someone displays trust in you and confides in you, don't disappoint her by violating her faith and confidence in you.

To Meet People, Go Where You Have Fun

There are countless places to meet people, and there is little doubt that some places are better than others, especially to make contact with someone special. The "right place" could be a social event, church, political gathering, or even an adult education class. If you have a mutual interest, you're in the right place. When you meet someone in a place where you both enjoy the activities, you already have something in common and can begin developing a friendship.

Meet People Who Have Similar Interests

Suppose you are a beginning photographer, and you like to take rides into the country to shoot pictures. You have just gotten a new camera, and now you have decided to sign up for a beginning photography class. At the photography class, you will meet other people with at least one thing in common—photography. Many of your early conversations will probably focus around this topic and other related fields. Start your conversations by finding out the different reasons others are taking the class. You can ask questions like: "What do you hope to gain from this class?" or "How long have you been taking photographs?" or "How did you become interested in photography?" As you talk, you can get a sense of whether you and the other person enjoy each other's company. If so, you may have started a new friendship.

New Friendships Can Begin Anywhere

Think of all the people you meet and see at work, in your neighborhood, and especially at recreational or social events you attend. Many are potential friends and you can develop relationships with them.

Become Familiar with People

When you see the same people over a period of time, you can start conversations. Find out if you have something in common and, if the conditions are right, start up a friendship. Becoming familiar with the people you see often will make this much easier. Start by smiling and saying hello and, if the opportunity arises, introduce yourself.

Keep It Friendly—Nothing Too Heavy or Too Serious

After you have said hello a few times, you will most likely find an opportunity to stop and chat for a few moments. Maybe it's at work, walking down the street, or in the local food store. Show the other person that you are interested in getting to know him better by engaging in casual conversation. You don't have to be profound or too impressive. It's better to be informal, friendly, and receptive. *Remember:* Small talk sends the signal: "I'm interested in you, and open to conversation. Let's talk!"

Use Ritual Questions to Send the Message: "I Want to Get to Know You Better"

How long have you been working here?
Have you lived in this neighborhood for a long time?
Where did you live before?
How did you get involved in this kind of work?
What do you like to do around here for entertainment?

These ritual questions signal your interest, and give the other person the opportunity to express interest in you. As the person speaks, listen for free information, and pick up on these topics. Ask yourself: "Do I want to get to know this person better?"

Zero in on "Hot Buttons"

The sooner you find out what turns someone on, the sooner you'll be able to establish whether you have anything in common. Sometimes you will know about a person before you actually meet. Remember to look for objects that the person carries, such as store bags, roller skates, an artist's portfolio, or anything that might give you a clue to the person's hot button. Then ask, "I saw you walking the other day with a large bag of groceries. Do you like to cook?"

Keep an Inventory of Facts and Details About the Person

When you talk to someone and recall information he gave you in a previous conversation, he will be surprised and flattered. Comments like "How's the job hunt going?" or "How's your garden coming along?" will show the other person that you were actually listening and that you care about what's happening in his life. This makes the person feel good—and important.

Be sure to concentrate on the details that someone discloses to you, and make a point to remember key words and free information he provides. You'll be able to draw on this reservoir of information to sustain and direct later conversations.

Making the Other Person Feel Important

When you remember details about the people you meet, you make them feel special. Your attention demonstrates your interest and curiosity, and encourages them to talk and reveal more information. When people begin to open up, it shows they are gaining trust in you and are comfortable with you.

Don't Wait to Introduce Yourself

When there is a pause in conversation, take the opportunity to say, "By the way, my name is _____. What's yours?" The sooner you introduce yourself, the easier it is. Remember, the longer you wait to make an introduction, the more uncomfortable it can get.

Show You Like the Other Person

When you want to make friends with someone, let her know you like her and want to get to know her better. Make it a point to stop and chat when the opportunity presents itself. You will be reinforcing a friendly, outgoing attitude. When you show a person that you like her, she will usually respond in a friendly manner.

Caution: Take care not to come on too strong to someone you have recently met. Be casual, informal, and comfortable. Take it slow and easy, and don't be pushy or aggressive.

"How About Meeting Sometime for a Drink or a Cup of Coffee?"

During casual conversation with someone you want to become better acquainted with, suggest going out for some casual conversation over a drink, coffee, ice cream, or any other informal activity. This shows you like the person and want to spend time with him. If the person is available (there may be a boyfriend or girlfriend to answer to) and receptive, chances are she may say, "Sure, why not!" Make an attempt to set a particular day and time by saying, "What's a good day and time for you?" or "How's tonight?" or "When's good for you?"

FAQ

I'm at work talking to a friend. I want to have dinner with him, but I'm afraid to ask. What should I do?

Getting someone to share a meal with you isn't really so difficult when you figure nearly everybody eats at least one meal daily. When you are speaking to someone you already know slightly, at work or in any other situation, keep your ears open for a "food" hot button. It's easy to introduce the subject into conversation by merely asking questions about nearby restaurants, particular favorite foods, or memorable meals. Say: "Do you know any good restaurants around here?" or "How is the food at the restaurant on the corner?" or "Have you ever been to Louie's? I hear the food there is excellent!"

Once you establish that you have some similar tastes in food, then suggest, "How about meeting for dinner one night next week after work? I know a great little place with great food and a fantastic atmosphere."

Usually if someone wants to spend time with you he will accept your open invitation. Now it's up to you to focus on a specific day and time. "What are you doing for dinner tonight? Are you interested in _____ food?" is an easy way to ask someone to share a meal with you. If you expect to be taken out for dinner, then you will have to wait for an invitation. If you go dutch treat, there are no expectations attached, and either party can initiate the date.

Plan an Activity Around a Mutual Interest

After you spend some time together informally, propose sharing a longer activity you know the other person likes to do, and one that you are interested in, too. It could be going to a movie, bike riding, or going out to dinner. It won't matter as long as the event is mutually interesting, and the focus is on fun. Presenting a few options and suggesting a date within the next week or so will increase the likelihood of a positive response. Your invitation could open with something like:

"I remember when we talked before that you said you liked (the activity), so I was wondering, are you interested in joining me for . . .

. . . dinner one night this weekend?"
. . . a movie this weekend?"
. . . Sunday's baseball game?"
. . . an art exhibition Thursday at the museum?"
. . . a few sets of tennis after work?"
. . . a walk on the beach?"
. . . a bike ride?"
. . . a class on the Internet?"

"Hi, Karen, This Is Don. Do You Have a Few Minutes?"

Give your friend a call to confirm the time of your planned meeting, and just to say hello. Here are some tips for more comfortable telephone conversations.

- Get comfortable—preferably seated.
- When the person answers the phone, always identify yourself and *never play* "Guess who this is." Say, "Hi _____, this is _____. Have you got a few minutes to talk?"
- Ask a detail about some aspect of the person's life, like "How's the writing coming along?" or "How did you make out with the job interview?"
- Tell the other person why you are calling. "I just wanted to confirm our meeting" or "I just thought I'd call to say hi."
- End your telephone call with a friendly comment like, "It's been nice talking with you," or "We'll be talking again soon," or "I'm looking forward to getting together with you on Saturday."

Maintain Contact with People You Like

Once you've made contact with someone you like and find activities that you enjoy doing together, then continue to maintain contact so the friendship can grow. As time goes on, you and your friend can contact each other anytime you want companionship, assistance, or advice.

When you are asked to join an activity by someone, make an all-out effort to accept the invitation. This reinforces the other person's feelings of friendship toward you, and encourages her to share her experiences and activities. When you hear yourself say, "I really don't feel like it," this translates as disinterest. If you decline too many invitations, the other person will get the message that you're not interested in getting together.

Be Open to New Experiences from Others

Let your friends introduce you to new places, people, food, or anything else they want to share. This projects openness and receptivity to your friends' ideas, and allows them to feel good about sharing things they enjoy. This attitude creates a positive feeling toward you, and your friends will become more receptive to the ideas and activities you suggest.

Share Activities with Your Friends

Take the initiative and ask your friends to share in activities that you enjoy, too. Make an effort to share some of the special places and events that interest you. This provides an opportunity for you to show others you like them, and reveals more information about you in subtle and indirect ways. Initiating an activity also gives you greater control over the direction of the event and the surrounding conversation.

Friendships Grow and Develop in Time

Sometimes friendships are like plants—they can grow slowly and steadily in time. Your friendship will grow as you share more experiences together. Time and shared experiences are important elements in friendships and can be expressed in these ways:

We've been good friends for a long time.
We've gone through some pretty amazing times together.
I don't know what I would have done without you.
I want to thank you for all the help and support you've given me during the last couple of months. It's really made a big difference, and I appreciate it a lot.

These last few months that we have spent together have been really fun. I've enjoyed them a lot!

FAQ

I'm with an old friend whom I haven't seen for a long time. Where does the conversation begin?

When talking with old friends, it's important to reestablish old ties and bring each other up to date. Since there are many changes in our lives that happen over time, focus on the big events in your life. Talk about situations where you will be making decisions in the near future, and bounce your ideas off on your friend for feedback. This will help your decision-making process, and will also deepen your relationship.

It is equally important to seek out similar information from your friend. Chances are things have developed for him as well, and you may have to encourage him to talk about it. Find out how he feels about what he is doing, where he is going, or whom he is involved with.

Sometimes old relationships need a little "priming" to get the words flowing again. However, once you get over those early feelings of "What can I say to this person that he doesn't already know about me?" the conversation will usually flow naturally.

"The Only Way to Have a Friend Is to Be One"

—Ralph Waldo Emerson

It has been said that a friend knows all about you, but likes you anyway. For people to remain friends and friendships to grow requires flexibility and tolerance. Accept your friends as unique individuals with all the problems, hang-ups, and inconsistencies that all humans possess. If you accept your friends on these conditions, you will be much more likely to keep them. Do what you can for your friends, and when you are asked for a favor, then do it if you possibly can. It all comes back to you in friendship. If you are a good friend, you'll have good friends.

Friends Grow Together

When people find common interests they can develop individually as well as together; sharing these interests can enrich their lives and experiences. Developing and learning together is one of the most gratifying aspects of a relationship. In the best friendships, developing, learning, and laughing never stop.

Part IV

*Boosting Your
Conversations to
the Next Level*

9

Recognizing and Using
Conversation Styles

I've told you a million times not to talk to me when I'm
doing my lashes.
                        —Jean Harlow (1911–1937),
                        in the 1933 movie *Dinner at Eight*

Do some of your conversations start with a bang while others sputter out after a few uncomfortable moments? Once you begin talking, do some of your chats flow smoothly from topic to topic, while others degenerate into heated disagreements? Is it a mystery why one discussion is fun and stimulating, while another is interminably boring? Are some folks just easier to talk to than others? In a nutshell, are your conversations something like playing roulette in that you're never sure if you are going to come out a winner or a loser?

One way to minimize conversational ups and downs is to recognize and use conversation styles. Most people have a primary conversation style that loosely falls into one of four categories. (You'll know your conversation style after you take the short self-assessment on the next few pages.) By identifying your own style, plus recognizing the strengths and weaknesses of each of the four styles, you can feel more comfortable while talking to almost anyone. You will see how quickly you can create rapport and skillfully converse with nearly everyone you meet—no matter how different his or her style is from yours. Besides building your confidence, you can mingle more easily with groups, quickly find common ground with strangers, and make plenty of new friends.

What's Your Conversation Style?

Answer the following questions to identify your primary conversation style. Choose the letter that best describes how you truly behave—not how you'd like to behave—in each situation.

1. When I enter a roomful of strangers I:
   ❑ a. mingle and observe interesting discussions. ♥
   ❑ b. introduce myself to the first stranger I meet. ♠
   ❑ c. sit in a chair and wait for someone to approach me. ♦
   ❑ d. look for a "friendly debate." ♣

2. When I meet people for the first time I:
   ❑ a. wait a little while before I form my opinions of them. ♥
   ❑ b. tell them about me before I ask my questions. ♣
   ❑ c. try to make them laugh. ♠
   ❑ d. play it cool and see what they do. ♦

3. When I am engaged in conversation I:
   ❑ a. let others share their opinions before I offer my own. ♦
   ❑ b. listen for holes in the other person's opinions. ♥
   ❑ c. get my point across as quickly as I can. ♣
   ❑ d. ask questions and share my views. ♠

4. If I am uninformed about a topic of conversation I:
- ❑ a. nod silently and try to look interested. ♦
- ❑ b. change the subject. ♥
- ❑ c. ask questions to show interest. ♠
- ❑ d. pretend like I know what I'm talking about. ♠

5. If I disagree with another person's views I:
- ❑ a. ask for the reasons behind his opinion. ♠
- ❑ b. excuse myself from the conversation as quickly as possible. ♦
- ❑ c. vigorously press my opinion until she agrees with me. ♣
- ❑ d. explain point by point why he is wrong. ♥

6. I prefer conversations that are:
- ❑ a. to the point. ♣
- ❑ b. factual and detailed. ♥
- ❑ c. oriented around "small talk." ♠
- ❑ d. personal. ♦

7. I like conversations that allow me to:
- ❑ a. learn about others. ♦
- ❑ b. be the center of attention. ♠
- ❑ c. explain complicated concepts. ♥
- ❑ d. tell others what I have accomplished. ♣

8. Which statement best describes you?
- ❑ a. I can make "small talk" about a variety of subjects. ♠
- ❑ b. I can zero in on the core issue of a topic. ♣
- ❑ c. I can listen so that others will open up to me. ♦
- ❑ d. I can explain difficult concepts. ♥

9. The people who I find hardest to talk with are those who:
- ❑ a. push their opinions on me. ♦
- ❑ b. speak nonstop without letting anyone else get a word in edgewise. ♥
- ❑ c. get hung up on every little detail. ♣
- ❑ d. don't smile and say very little. ♠

10. My favorite conversations are the ones in which I:
- ❑ a. tell a funny story. ♠
- ❑ b. discuss a technical topic. ♥
- ❑ c. present a viewpoint. ♣
- ❑ d. listen to others open up. ♦

Scoring

Count the number of responses with each of the symbols (♠ ♦ ♣ ♥). The style with the *highest* number of responses is probably closest to your conversation style. Most people are a combination of styles with one or sometimes two primary styles. Since there are ten questions, your total will add up to 10.

For example:		**Your scores:**	
♣ ___6___	Candid	♣ _____	Candid
♦ ___0___	Hang Back	♦ _____	Hang Back
♥ ___1___	Accurate	♥ _____	Accurate
♠ ___3___	Talkative	♠ _____	Talkative
Total ___10___		Total ___10___	

What else do the numbers mean?

If you scored:
8–10 (high) you have a strong tendency to always communicate in this style.

3–7 (middle) you can easily shift into this conversation style from other styles.

0–2 (low) you rarely communicate in this style and might find it difficult to talk to people who converse in this style.

Understanding and Using Different Conversation Styles

I like to think of conversation like dancing. Each person I talk (or dance) with is a new partner with a different conversation style. One partner may be outgoing while the other is reserved. One may prefer heated political discussions while the other enjoys comparing movie reviews. You can use the letters in *C-H-A-T* to help you remember how to adjust your conversation style so you can "dance" with everyone you meet.

Each Letter in the Word C-H-A-T Stands for One of Four Chatting Styles

C=Candid
H=Hang Back
A=Accurate
T=Talkative

C Stands for CANDID (♣)

If most of your answers fell into the CANDID category, you have a straightforward approach to conversation.

Your Conversational Strengths

You usually say what's on your mind without mincing words. You most likely thrive on competition of all kinds and often see conversation as a jousting match in which you have the opportunity to debate, argue, or convince someone of your opinion. You love to "mix it up," conversationally speaking, and are fun and beneficial to chat with if people share your sense of humor, intensity, and competitiveness.

Your Conversational Weaknesses

Because you're keenly competitive, you see conversations as a match that you must "win." As a result, others often describe you as blunt, pushy, or too aggressive. You have a tendency to get impatient with people who have a less energetic or direct style. Your habit of "shooting from the lip" often ignores how your directness affects others. People feel that you are at times domineering, boastful, or tactless.

People with a Candid Chatting Style May Like to Talk About:

☆ sports ☆ crime ☆ business heroes ☆ adventure stories ☆ action movies ☆ politics ☆ entrepreneurial endeavors ☆ money & power ☆ military experiences ☆ working out

---

If you scored *low* in this category, follow these Dos & Don'ts when talking to people with the CANDID style:

Do show a genuine interest in their business and personal goals.

These folks love to talk about themselves and their achievements.

Don't get into any debates with them even if they challenge your opinions.

They like arguing, are good at it, and usually win.

Do ask for their opinions and advice.

You can learn a lot from these goal-oriented people.

Don't go into overly detailed or complex explanations.

They are "big picture" thinkers who get impatient discussing minor details.

Do show a self-effacing sense of humor.

They like others who are not afraid of laughing at themselves.

Don't take offense if they heckle you or belittle your accomplishments.

Teasing and put-downs are their way of testing your level of self-confidence.

H Stands for HANG BACK (♦)

If most of your answers fell into the HANG BACK category, you have a reserved approach to conversation.

Your Conversational Strengths

Thoughtful is the word that describes your conversation style. You are soft-spoken and calm when you do talk. Since your style is nonthreatening, others will open up to you. As a rule, you are an excellent listener and sympathetic to the feelings of others, especially to those you already have met. It takes you a little time, but once you get to know a person, you open up and converse easily.

Your Conversational Weaknesses

Your tendency to remain passive gives others the often false impression that you are shy, disinterested, snobbish, or unwilling to communicate. You often get overwhelmed by aggressive or talkative types, and clam up when you feel anxious. Your fear of saying the wrong thing, being boring, or offending others inhibits your spontaneity and often makes the first few minutes of your conversations awkward.

> ### People with a HANG BACK Chatting Style May Like to Talk About:
>
> ☆ relationships ☆ human interest stories ☆ personal stories ☆ movie stars ☆ food ☆ cooking & restaurants ☆ home decorating ☆ art ☆ music ☆ theater ☆ poetry ☆ dance ☆ books ☆ social issues ☆ hobbies ☆ gardening ☆ animals ☆ family

If you scored *low* in this category, follow these Dos and Don'ts when talking to people with a HANG BACK style:

Do show a desire to talk about their interests.
These folks need a little extra encouragement to open up.
Don't get aggressive, critical, or argumentative.
They turn off almost immediately at the first sign of conflict.
Do ask for their views, feelings, and insight about issues that concern people.
They will open up if you let them know you value what they have to say.
Don't interrupt them or complete their sentences.
These people often pause to consider their words, so give them time to finish speaking.

Do encourage them to talk by emphasizing common views and interests.

Your interested response is essential for them to reveal their opinions.

Don't give up when the conversation takes a little more time to get going.

People with this style take their time before opening up to strangers.

A Stands for ACCURATE (♥)

If most of your answers fell into the ACCURATE category, you have a methodical approach to conversation.

Your Conversational Strengths

Your ability to absorb, assess, and impart information helps you converse about technical topics such as computers, engineering, or other detail- or process-oriented subjects. Your ability to break down procedures from the first detail, then to the next, all the way through to the finish, without skipping any points along the way helps you explain difficult concepts. You enjoy "shop talk" and more serious subjects that require detailed knowledge or problem solving.

Your Conversational Weaknesses

You rarely are the one to "break the ice," so others may see you as shy or unavailable for conversation. Your tendency to go into excruciating detail about specific topics can cause some people to lose interest or become confused about your main point. Your logical approach can give the impression that you have little patience for others who do not understand technical or complicated subjects or think differently than you. You can come across to others as overly serious because you tend to avoid making "small talk."

**People with an ACCURATE Chatting Style
May Like to Talk About:**

☆ science & math ☆ architecture ☆ computers ☆ design ☆ stock markets ☆ technology ☆ how things work ☆ inventions ☆ science fiction/fantasy ☆ mysteries ☆ home improvement & tools

---

If you scored *low* in this category, follow these Dos and Don'ts when talking to people with an ACCURATE style:

Do praise their technical knowledge.

These people like to impress others with their intelligence, so let them.

Don't get into debates or contradict their views.

They hate being wrong and take criticism personally.

Do encourage them to talk about subjects outside their specific area of expertise.

"Bridge" your conversation to related subjects or look forward to hearing everything you never wanted to know about computer hard drives, pumps, or who knows what else.

Don't change topics too frequently.

People with this style prefer to limit the discussion to one topic at a time.

Do gently change the conversation to lighter topics of interest.

These folks have a tendency to dwell on serious or tedious topics for too long.

Don't be offended if you hear criticism or offers of unsolicited advice.

They see everything as a "problem" to be solved and they want to have all the answers.

T Stands for TALKATIVE (♠)

If most of your answers fell into the TALKATIVE category, you have an outgoing approach to conversation.

Your Conversational Strengths

You've probably been accused more than once to have been "vaccinated with a phonograph needle." You're an extroverted, energetic conversationalist who can talk about anything, as long as you have an audience. You thoroughly enjoy interacting with others and being the center of attention. You're perfectly happy to initiate conversations with just about anyone. People see you as a fun and friendly person who is open to contact.

Your Conversational Weaknesses

You can talk too much. Less talkative styles sometimes feel overwhelmed when they talk with you because you come across to these people as overbearing. Your tendency to dominate the conversation and be the center of attention makes others feel left out. You sometimes fail to listen or give others a chance to participate.

People with a TALKATIVE Chatting Style May Like to Talk About:

☆ themselves ☆ friends & family ☆ travel ☆ food & entertainment ☆ pop culture ☆ hobbies ☆ self-improvement ☆ successful people ☆ unusual media stories ☆ humorous events ☆ their hopes & dreams ☆ pets ☆ just about anything that isn't technical or complicated

---

If you scored *low* in this category, follow these Dos and Don'ts when talking to people with a TALKATIVE style:

Do let them have center stage.

They crave recognition and attention, so show you appreciate their efforts.

Don't get into detailed explanations about technical topics or difficult concepts.

They'll just get confused, frustrated, and bored.

Do share your interests with them.

If you don't, they'll talk your ear off.

Don't feel bad when you interrupt them to speak.

If you don't speak up, you will never get a word in edgewise.

Do be playful, show your sense of humor, and above all, laugh at their jokes.

They really want others to like them and think that they are funny.

Don't discuss heavy topics or get too serious.

Having fun in a conversation is one of their top priorities.

Blend the Four Styles to be a Well-Rounded Conversationalist

While most people seem to lean toward one conversation style, they probably have a few strengths and weaknesses from each of the four styles. Here are four ways to help blend your style with the other three styles and improve your conversations with practically everyone you talk to.

☞ Recognize your strengths and weaknesses in each of the styles.

☞ Build on your strengths and eliminate your weaknesses from each style.

☞ Adjust your conversational style to "dance" with the styles of others.

☞ Practice chatting with people whose style is different from your own.

FAQ

How do you immediately recognize the conversation style of a stranger?

You'll soon recognize the conversation style of strangers when you pay close attention to body language and how the first few minutes of the conversation progress. Is she outgoing or shy? Does he like to make small talk or only "shop talk?" Is she to the point or reserved? Is he argumentative or easygoing?

Make it a habit to observe the four styles as you talk to the people around you at work, home, the store—everywhere! In no time, your success will soar when talking to new and old acquaintances. Plus, you'll have a lot more fun on those "spins" around the conversational dance floor.

10

Talking to People from Other Countries

Guides cannot master the subtleties of the American joke.
—Mark Twain (1835–1910),
a.k.a. Samuel Clemens, writer, humorist

Do you know how to talk and act with people from other countries without offending them, being offended, or putting yourself into embarrassing situations? Since friendliness and good intentions may not always bridge the gap that exists between cultures, remember these dos and don'ts when speaking to people whose backgrounds and cultures differ from your own.

Do respect differences.
Don't be shy about introducing yourself.
Do show interest in the other person's country.
Don't take offense if someone says the wrong thing.
Do avoid stereotyping.
Don't assume you know the country a person is from.
Do match your speaking speed and vocabulary with the person's language skills.
Don't assume understanding.
Do talk about upbeat topics.
Don't talk about depressing topics.

Do Respect Differences

Many countries around the world have become "melting pots" of cultures, and today's society has more diverse traditions, religions, and ethnic groups than ever before. By assuming that people from other countries share your values, attitudes, and ways of communicating, you can fall into social blunders or uncomfortable conversations. However, if you remember that people from different countries frequently have different styles of talking and acting, then you'll be less likely to be offended or give offense.

FAQ

Is it true that Americans are more informal than people from other countries?

Although Americans are known for their friendliness, their informality isn't always appreciated or understood by people from other countries. "Coming on too strong, too soon" is a common complaint heard about Americans by those who prefer a more formal manner with people they don't know well. In general, use a more reserved conversation style when you meet people from countries other than the United States.

Don't Be Shy about Introducing Yourself

"Hello, my name is Don Gabor" is a perfectly acceptable way to start conversations with foreigners in most social and business situations. This friendly and typically American greeting shows others that you want to talk to them. While etiquette experts still frown upon using someone's first name before being given permission, most Americans seem to do it any-way. However, many British, Europeans, Middle Easterners, and Asians prefer to use their titles (Mr., Mrs., Miss, or Dr.) and last names when they talk to new acquaintances. Although the custom of shaking hands when meeting a stranger is a generally accepted practice in most countries, there are many exceptions. The chart in the next chapter shows you customary ways to greet people from various countries around the world.

Tip on Remembering Foreign or Uncommon Names

When a name is unfamiliar or difficult to pronounce, ask the person to spell it for you and to say it correctly. Picture what the letters spell phonetically or sound similar to. For example, if you meet Vanya Roussetzki, think: Vawn-ya Rose-ETZ-skee. It may take you several times to get it right, but most foreigners feel flattered when you use and remember their names.

After chatting for a while, you may feel like the time is right to move to a first-name basis. Then you can say, "Please call me (your first name)." Depending on the other person's pref-erence and the situation, he may follow your lead. If not, con-tinue to use his title and last name until you are invited to do otherwise.

Do Show Interest in the Other Person's Country

Show genuine curiosity and interest in the other person's country by seeking general background information about his or her homeland. The more appreciation you show for her culture, the greater the likelihood she will open up and talk to you. As you talk, listen and observe carefully for topics and behaviors to expand upon and those to avoid. Find out all you can about her country, town, people, food, music, and so on, and you will have plenty of conversational fuel. Always take care to steer clear of conversations about sex, politics, and religion. These traditional "taboo topics" are highly charged and can lead to disagreements. However, you can feel free to ask more ritual, information-seeking questions such as:

Tell me a little about the town where you are from.
What's it like where you grew up (used to live, etc.)?
What kinds of work do people do where you live?
Is your town or area known for any special tourist attractions?
What kinds of things do people in your town do for fun?

While many people from foreign countries like to practice their English, they are usually delighted if you ask them to teach you a few ritual phrases in their native language. This technique is a great way to build rapport and show appreciation for their country and culture. For example, you can ask, "How do you say 'Hello,' 'Good-bye,' 'Please,' 'Thank you,' and 'How are you?' in Greek (Japanese, Polish, etc.)?" Then, when you see the person the next time, say a few words in his language and watch his smile and eyes light up!

Don't Take Offense if Someone Says the Wrong Thing

What should you say if a foreigner makes a sweeping generalization about your country or the place where you live, and you don't agree? First, don't take offense or start to argue. Instead, you can say something like, "It might appear that way to you, but I don't think most people who live here share that view, myself included."

With the many regional differences that exist in most countries, it comes as no surprise that newcomers may not be tuned into local customs or etiquette. Questions that you might consider personal, such as "How much money do you make?" or "Why don't you have any children?" might be perfectly acceptable in the other person's homeland.

Rather than be offended by personal questions, view them as a genuine curiosity about your lifestyle and culture. You can offer a general response, such as "People in my profession earn anywhere between . . . , depending on their education and experience" or "There are lots of married couples in this country who don't have children, and I'm sure that they all have their own reasons." If the person presses the point, and you don't want to be more specific, say, "Most people here consider questions like that personal, so I'd rather not say," or "That's a topic that I don't feel comfortable discussing."

Do Avoid Stereotyping

Although people from particular countries or regions around the world often share similar customs and conversational styles, resist the urge to lump everyone together with generalized statements. Never stereotype people with comments such as "You French (Germans, Chinese, Indians, or whoever) always . . ." Better conversations develop with people from other countries when you ask them for their individual opinions, views, and feelings.

Don't Assume You Know the Country a Person Is From

"You're not from England? But you sound so English!" This conversational blunder happens a lot to people who speak with what sounds like a British accent. In fact, they may be from South Africa, New Zealand, Australia, Ireland, Scotland, Wales, India, Canada, Ghana, Belize, Hong Kong, Zimbabwe, or any other of the fifty independent nations or protectorates that were once British colonies.

People are usually offended if you make incorrect assumptions about their nationality based on their appearance, language, or accent. For example, French—the mother tongue of more than 90 million people around the globe—is spoken in Quebec, Haiti, Guinea, Indochina, Morocco, Algeria, and several other countries in the Caribbean and North Africa. Spanish is the most widely spoken Romance language in the world. It is the official language of Spain and most of Latin America, with more than 14.5 million Spanish-speaking people in the United States, many of whom are American-born. Assuming that a person is from Mexico, for example, because she speaks Spanish could be embarrassing.

English-speaking Canadians dislike being taken for Americans, although it happens all the time. French Canadians will fiercely correct anyone who suggests that they are from France. Asians of one nationality are greatly offended if they are confused with Asians of another nationality. You could start a small war if you confuse a Greek and a Turk, or an Israeli with a Palestinian. Like other examples of cultural faux pas, the list goes on and on.

Avoid assumptions about people's origins by carefully listening for any geographical references that might provide clues as to where their homeland is. If you hear a particular city name, for example, you can ask, "You went to school in Hong Kong? Is that where you are from?" If you're not sure, avoid the tendency to guess. It is okay to be direct and ask, "Where are you from?" or "Where did you grow up?" or "Where were you born?"

Do Match Your Speaking Speed and Vocabulary with the Person's Language Skills

Let's face it. Learning a new language is tough, especially with all the slang, idioms, abbreviations, and jargon that fill daily conversations. When you first meet someone whose native language is not your own, speak slowly and keep your sentences short until you can determine his or her level of understanding. If there is a language barrier, be patient and follow one international host's excellent advice: "Keep it simple, don't talk loudly, and never act like you are speaking to a child."

Be aware that many people feel self-conscious about their ability to speak a foreign language and may need a little extra encouragement from you to carry on a conversation. If the person suggests that his or her language skills are inadequate, you can say, "I think you speak quite well! How long have you been studying the language?"

Don't Assume Understanding

Over the course of your conversation, be sure to check that the other person understands you. Even when they don't fully comprehend your meaning or intent, people with limited foreign language skills often nod their heads or say "Yes" if you ask, "Do you understand?"

You can avoid many misunderstandings by asking questions that require the other person to restate, or paraphrase, what you have said. For example, you can say, "Just to make sure you understand how to find our house, why don't you repeat the directions to me." Or you can restate what you think he or she has said. For example, "I just want to make sure that I understand you correctly. You want me to . . . Is that right?"

If you find that your message did not get through, then try restating it more directly and in fewer words. You can say, "Let me say it a different way."

FAQ

I know to avoid discussing sex, politics, and religion, but what topics are okay to bring up when I'm talking with someone from another country?

Do Talk about Upbeat Topics

Most people from other countries enjoy exchanging views on a variety of subjects that reveal their interests, experiences, and tastes. For example, you can talk about:

American culture	Entrepreneurs	Outdoor activities
Animals	Family life*	Professions
Art	Fashion	Scenery/Geography
Business/Work	Food & Drink	Science/Technology
Cars	Gardening	Sports
City/country life	History*	Tourist attractions
Culture/Heritage	Hobbies	Travel
Current events*	Language	Volunteer work
Customs	Literature	Weather/Climate
Entertainment	Music	World affairs*

Caution: Take care when discussing these topics, as they can lead to strong differences of opinion or uncomfortable conversations.

Here are a few examples of how to start a conversation using some of these topics:

What are the surroundings like where you live back home? *(Scenery/Geography)*

What is your city or town like? *(City or country life)*

What do you find most interesting about life here? *(American culture)*

When you have time off from work, what do you like to do? *(Hobbies)*

Tell me a little about your town's history. *(Culture/ Heritage)*

How do you compare doing business here with doing it at home in your country? *(Business/Work)*

Have you recently seen any movies (plays, music, etc.) that you liked? *(Entertainment)*

If I were to visit your country (city, etc.), where would you suggest that I go? *(Travel)*

Who do you think is likely to win the World Cup (soccer) this year? *(Sports)*

Don't Talk about Depressing Topics

Avoid discussing the following topics with people from other countries until you know them better. These controversial topics can polarize people and put them into a somber mood, particularly in social or business situations.

Alcohol/Drug abuse	Ethnic humor	Radical unrest
Apartheid	Internal politics	Regional conflicts
Brutal crimes	Money problems	Religion
Cold War	Organized crime	Sex
Colonialism	Personal illness	Taxes
Communism	Politics	Terrorism
Economic problems	Poverty	Tragedies

FAQ

How do you sustain a friendship with someone from a different country?

Once you've met someone from another country, the next step is to build the friendship, and the key is to maintain contact. Send your new friend a letter or postcard to say how much you enjoyed meeting him and that you'd like to "stay in touch." Remembering his birthday or a special event will help cement the relationship. E-mail has made it possible to have nearly instant contact with people all over the world, so it's now easier than ever to be in contact. With some international long-distance telephone calling plans, you can talk to people thousands of miles away for reasonable rates. Of course, try to meet your friend in person whenever it's possible.

Conversing with People from Other Countries Builds Bridges of Friendship

Someone long ago once said that the world is like a book, and those who do not travel read only one page. Today, however, with so many people from around the world traveling or living abroad, you have the opportunity to meet foreigners in your hometown.

Discovering new foods, customs, music, business opportunities, perspectives, and values are only a few of the many benefits you have to gain from conversing with people from around the world. But the biggest reward of all when you meet and talk to people who are different than yourself is that of mutual understanding and international friendship.

11

Customs That Influence Cross-Cultural Conversations

The more I traveled, the more I realized that fear makes strangers of people who should be friends.
—Shirley MacLaine (1934–   ), American actress

I can't believe she asked me how much my engagement ring cost!" "Okay, so I'm five minutes late. What's the big deal?" "I wish that he wouldn't stand so close to me when we speak."

Talking to people from other countries can be challenging, especially when you have little knowledge of their cultural sensitivities and taboos. That's why the more you know about a person's culture and homeland, the less likely you will say the wrong thing or be offended by his or her customs.

How Savvy Are You about the Customs of Other Cultures?

Take this True/False quiz and find out how much you know about talking to people from other countries. The answers are on pages 164-67.

1. Japanese like a strong handshake when they meet strangers.   T__ F__
2. Being only a few minutes late to an appointment will upset a German.   T__ F__
3. North Americans stand closer than Latin Americans when they talk.   T__ F__

4. Chinese gesture with their hands when
   they speak.   T__ F__
5. Using first names is customary in the
   U.S., but considered rude by Europeans,
   Asians, and Latin Americans if done so
   without permission.   T__ F__
6. All cultures view lack of eye contact
   as a sign of dishonesty.   T__ F__
7. Women should offer to shake hands with
   men from the Middle East.   T__ F__
8. Bulgarians and Greeks nod their heads
   when they disagree.   T__ F__
9. South Americans consider it rude to back
   away in a conversation.   T__ F__
10. Italians never make small talk before
    bringing up business issues.   T__ F__
11. A woman from India would be offended
    if you pointed at her with your finger.   T__ F__
12. Africans enjoy talking about music, art,
    sculpture, and oral literature.   T__ F__
13. Filipinos rarely say no or argue
    with foreigners.   T__ F__
14. Casual and informal conversations are
    typical of most people from the Caribbean. T__ F__
15. The topic of soccer would bore most
    Central Americans.   T__ F__

Answers

1. False: Although Japanese are accustomed to shaking
   hands with Westerners, they prefer a light handshake.
2. True: Punctuality is of the upmost importance to Germans. They consider it rude when someone is even a

few minutes late to a business or social engagement.

3. False: North Americans prefer to stand about three feet from the people they speak with. Latin Americans speak at a distance of one to two feet.

4. False: Chinese rarely speak with their hands and find it distracting when speaking with people who do.

5. True: Americans love to use first names from the moment they are introduced, although many foreigners consider it to be too informal.

6. False: Mexicans, for example, often avert their eyes out of respect.

7. False: Strict religious rules prohibit Muslims and Orthodox Jews from having physical contact with the opposite sex in public.

8. True: Bulgarians and Greeks shake their heads from side to side when they mean yes and nod their heads when they mean no.

9. True: Backing away during a conversation is considered rude by South Americans because they like to stand very close while they chat.

10. False: Be prepared to make conversation about your family, travel, food, and so on before discussing any business matters with Italians.

11. True: People from India consider it rude to point with a finger. They point with their chins.

12. True: Africans like to discuss the influence of their traditional music, art, sculpture, and oral literature on jazz, blues, modern art, and modern dance.

13. True: Filipinos value harmony in conversations and consider the word "no" impolite.

14. True: People from the Caribbean usually have a more relaxed style of talking than do Americans, British, French, Spanish, or Dutch.

15. False: Central Americans are passionate about soccer, as are most Europeans, Mexicans, and South Americans.

How Do Your Skills Rate?

Number of correct answers	Level/Follow-up
13-15	**Super!** You know how to talk to just about anyone from anywhere. Dig even deeper to find out more about the many subcultures that exist within each country and culture.
9-12	**Pretty good!** You are aware of many foreign customs that influence conversation. Zero in on the many exceptions that exist within cultures, so you don't assume too much when talking to someone from a particular country.
5-8	**Okay, but . . .** You know enough about people from other countries to have a conversation, but you might find yourself saying something embarrassing or offensive. Ask them more questions about where they are from and some of their customs. Continue your conversations based on the information they tell you.
0-4	**Oops!** You are at risk of saying the wrong thing when you talk to people from other countries. Try

0-4 (continued)

to learn more about the cultures and customs of other countries so that when you converse you won't put your foot in your mouth. If you ask questions, show interest, listen carefully, and observe their behavior, you'll quickly improve.

Use the Following Chart to Avoid Embarrassing Situations and Taboo Topics

It is easy to misinterpret actions of acquaintances and friends from other countries if you are unaware of their particular communication styles, customs, and taboos. The following chart summarizes greetings, conversation styles, body language, plus certain actions and topics to avoid while socializing with people from various countries and regions of the world. These traits are generalizations and the list does not include all nationalities, but the information is representative of the people that you will most likely encounter at home, at work, and in business or social situations.

FAQ

Will making generalizations about the foreigners I meet make them feel like I don't see them as individuals?

It is always important not to stereotype the people you meet. Be aware that you are speaking with individuals and that there are many cultural variations within countries and regions. To avoid saying or doing the wrong thing, observe, listen, and follow the other person's lead as you meet and converse. And remember to always be polite, mind your manners and *never* say, "But I thought everyone from your country . . ."

Conversation Customs Chart

Country/Region	Handshake/Greeting	Conversation Style
Central Africa*	medium	polite/leisurely
North Africa*	medium (men only)	unhurried
South Africa*	medium	polite/formal
Brazil	medium	outgoing
Canada	medium	relaxed/polite
Caribbean*	medium	informal
Central America*	light	polite/formal
China*	light/bow	reserved
Eastern Europe*	firm	outgoing
England	light	formal
France	light	proud/formal
Germany	firm	practical/formal
Greece	light	laid-back
India*	medium (men only)	leisurely
Israel	medium (men only)	to the point
Italy	light	demonstrative
Japan	light	reserved
Mexico	medium	friendly
Middle East*	medium (men only)	unhurried
Philippines	firm	social/formal
Poland	medium	demonstrative
Russia*	medium	demonstrative
Scandinavia	firm	reserved/formal
South America*	light-medium	personal
Southeast Asia*	light/nod	reserved
United States	firm	friendly/informal

* These countries and regions are ethnically diverse with a wide variety of cultures and customs.

Eye Contact	Standing Distance	Taboo Actions/Topics
medium	2-3 ft.	religion/political conflicts
medium	1-2 ft.	Middle East politics
medium	2-3 ft.	apartheid
strong	1-2 ft.	backing away
medium	3 ft.	mistaken for American
medium	2 ft.	drug trade
strong	1-2 ft.	backing away
light	3-4 ft.	mistaken for Japanese
medium	2-3 ft.	Communist rule
light	3 ft.	standing too close
strong	1-2 ft.	criticizing
medium	2-3 ft.	World War II
medium	2-3 ft.	refusing food
medium	2-3 ft.	saying "no"
medium	1-2 ft.	World War II
medium	1-2 ft.	Mafia
light	3-4 ft.	mistaken for Chinese
medium-light	1-2 ft.	backing away
strong	1-2 ft.	eating with left hand
light	2-3 ft.	hands on hips
medium	2-3 ft.	World War II
medium	1-2 ft.	criticizing
strong	2-3 ft.	loud outbursts
strong	1-2 ft.	backing away
limited	3-4 ft.	confrontation
medium	2-3 ft.	criticizing

More Ways to Learn about the Customs of People from Other Countries

In addition to talking to people about their homelands, you can take advantage of the many opportunities where you live to learn about other countries and cultures.

Visit or Attend

- ✔ Restaurants that serve food from other countries or cultures.
- ✔ Cultural events that feature music, dance, art, and food.*
- ✔ Cultural centers related to a particular country or culture.
- ✔ Foreign language classes.*
- ✔ International centers and volunteer to tutor people who want to learn your language.
- ✔ Lectures or classes about a country's customs or culture.*
- ✔ Museums that feature art from other countries.
- ✔ Folk dance classes or music classes.*
- ✔ Libraries where you can research places that you've always wanted to visit.

Read about other countries in

- ✔ *National Geographic* magazine.
- ✔ Travel and food sections of newspapers and magazines.
- ✔ Travel guides such as *Fodor's, Frommer's, Insight, Michelin,* or *The Rough Guides.*
- ✔ Newspaper features or human interest stories.
- ✔ Nonfiction or photography books.

---

* Of course, in addition to learning more about a particular country or culture, many of these places provide a great opportunity to meet people and make new friends!

✔ Novels that are set in and have characters from other countries.

Watch movies or television programs from other countries that

✔ Show how people live there.

✔ Present history and cultural development.

✔ Reveal historical perspectives about the people who live there.

✔ Discuss popular sporting events.

Web Sites

The Internet offers an endless source of information about most countries, including local cultural events. Once you are on-line, visit any search engine and type the name of the country that you want to know more about into the search box. You'll be amazed at how much you can learn when you browse these sites. Many web sites have bulletin boards where you can post messages and chat rooms where you can participate in on-line discussions.

Respectful Conversations Yield International Friendships

Adding new knowledge, respect, and tolerance for individual differences is the key to communicating effectively with foreigners. Every social and business situation holds the potential for rewarding conversations that allow the people from varying cultures to talk and learn about each other. As you become more comfortable with different communication styles, body language, customs, and taboos, many of your conversations will lead you to new friends from around the world.

12

Five Golden Rules of Mobile Phone Etiquette

> ET phone home.
> —from the movie *ET: The Extra-Terrestrial*

What do Buck Rogers, Dick Tracy, and millions of teenagers, parents, and businesspeople in the country have in common? They all use mobile phones (or, in the cases of Buck Rogers and Dick Tracy, the two-way wrist-radio version of a mobile phone) to stay in touch with their friends, family, and colleagues. What was once the dream of science-fiction writers is now a ringing reality for millions of people around the world. Parents use mobile phones to keep tabs on their children. Companies buy them for their employees so they are in constant contact with clients. Friends and lovers are never out of touch when they have their mobile phones turned on. Even clothes have special pockets to hold mobile phones for fast and easy access.

Whether you love or loathe this electronic communication gadget, using it thoughtfully can enhance your contact with the people you talk to every day. On the other hand, ignoring mobile phone etiquette can offend old friends, family, or colleagues, and even throw cold water on a new friendship.

Mobile Phones Are a Spontaneous Way to Build Friendships

If you are on the run these days more than ever, using a mobile phone is a convenient way to arrange an impromptu meeting. A quick call to an acquaintance is a great way to show that you are interested in spending more time with him or her and want to build the friendship. You might say something like, "Hello Jan, this is Cortez. I'm on my way to your neighborhood and I was wondering if you're free for lunch. How about meeting me for a quick bite?"

Tell Your Friend, "I'm on My Way."

Have you ever waited on a street corner or at a restaurant for a friend, family member, or colleague who is late? You're sure you agreed to meet at 6:00 P.M., right after work, and here it is 6:30 and he's nowhere in sight. Maybe he had to work late or is stuck in traffic. Or maybe he just forgot! How aggravating! Showing up a half hour late for a date—even with a good friend—can really hurt a relationship. But there is a solution to this problem if the other person has a mobile phone.

Is there a good chance that you'll be more than ten minutes late to an appointment? That's the moment to pull out your mobile phone and make a call to show that you respect the other person's time. All you need to say is something like, "Sorry, but I'm running about a half hour behind schedule. Is it okay if we meet about six-thirty instead of six o'clock?"

Making a Quick Change of Plans Is Easy on a Mobile Phone

If you're the one who's doing the waiting, then use your mobile phone to call your friend and check on what's happening. If you can see, for example, that now you won't have time to share dinner before going to a movie, suggest a change of plans and agree to meet at the theater. That way, you can have something to eat instead of waiting around for your late friend.

Five Golden Rules of Mobile Phone Etiquette

Just because you have a mobile phone doesn't mean that it's okay to use it anywhere or anytime that you like. Follow these golden rules and you'll be using your mobile phone the right way.

Golden Rule No. 1: Present Company Comes First

Remember that in most situations, the people you are with take precedence over the people you want to call or those who call you on your mobile phone. To avoid getting trapped into a long mobile phone conversation at an inconvenient time, simply tell the caller, "I can't talk right now. I'll call you back in an hour, if that's okay."

Golden Rule No. 2: Turn on "Vibrate" While Attending Social or Business Functions

This rule also applies when you are attending *any* public performance, such as a movie, concert, play, meeting, workshop, or lecture. Use the vibrate option on your mobile phone or call forwarding to reroute incoming calls to your voice mail. Check your messages if you must, but return the calls later.

Knowing When to Turn Off Your Mobile Phone Can Avoid an Embarrassing Moment

During a recent Broadway performance of the play *Death of a Salesman,* a mobile phone belonging to someone in the audience rang several times. After the fourth ring, Brian Dennehy, the Tony Award–winning star of the show, turned and shouted at the very embarrassed mobile phone owner, "Shut that damn thing off!"

Golden Rule No. 3: Choose the Right Time to Call

Avoid calling friends or family members who have mobile phones if you know they are attending a class, ceremony, concert, play, movie, or any other event where a ringing mobile phone would be an unwelcome interruption. Of course, mobile phones can save lives in an emergency, so always make that call if it's necessary.

Golden Rule No. 4: Find a Private or Semiprivate Place to Talk

No one wants to listen to your conversations or feel compelled to speak quietly because you're on your mobile phone. Look around for a bit of privacy before you make a call. Then chat on your mobile phone all you want to without annoying others.

Golden Rule No. 5: Speak at a Normal Volume

With loud street noise or other sounds in public places, you might find yourself speaking louder. If talking at a higher volume is necessary, try covering your mouth and mobile phone with your hand to muffle the sound of your voice.

FAQ

My new friend frequently gets into long conversations on her mobile phone when we go out to eat. How can I tell her that I think she is being rude to me and everyone else in the restaurant?

What could be more irritating than dining with someone in a restaurant who constantly carries on extended conversations on a mobile phone? Before ordering your meal, try saying something like this to your friend: "Can I ask you a little favor? Would you mind turning off your mobile phone while we are in the restaurant? I feel really embarrassed when you're on it talking to someone else and I'm sitting here twiddling my thumbs waiting for you to finish. Plus, I don't think it's fair to me or the other people here to have to listen to your conversation."

Conversation tip: Whenever you are criticizing a friend, state your complaint in a calm voice. Describe the undesirable behavior, how it affects you, and what you want him or her to do about it. Don't overdramatize the situation or make harsh accusations such as "You're so rude! Why do you always . . . ?" In most cases, a few well-spoken words at the right time will solve the problem. If your request goes unheeded, pull out a book or newspaper to keep busy while your dinner partner chats. Better still, find someone else to share your meal with or to talk to in the restaurant!

Mobile Phones Are a Great Way to Maintain Relationships

Mobile phones are a spontaneous and convenient way to communicate with old and new friends, family, and business contacts. Remember the five golden rules of mobile phone etiquette and all your conversations on the go will go great!

13

E-mail and On-line Chat Rooms: Making Conversation and Friends in Cyberspace

I chat therefore I am. Chatting is a way of life for me. Some of my closest friends are people whose faces I've not yet seen—all I know are their words.
—Julie Martin, about.com chat room host

Welcome to Twenty-First-Century Communications

In the old days (that is, prior to the Internet), people used to meet at school, work, in their neighborhood, where they worshiped, or where they played. If they hit it off, they exchanged telephone numbers and friendships began. Today, however, there is a new way for people to meet, make friends, and build their relationships. Welcome to the world of e-mail and on-line chat rooms. Communicating in cyberspace is already a way of life for lots of people. Why not log on, send an e-mail to an old buddy, and visit a chat room? See how easy it is to start a conversation and make new friends.

FAQ

I've heard that there are some rules to follow when using e-mail. What are they?

Five Ground Rules for Better E-mail

Most people agree that e-mail is the revolution of the 1990s, but many users don't know the basic ground rules. These rules will improve your e-mail messages to strangers, friends, relatives, acquaintances, and business contacts. They will help you avoid the most common mistakes that "newbies" (newcomers to the Internet) make when they use e-mail.

Ground Rule No. 1: Promptly Respond to E-mail Messages

An unanswered e-mail, like an unreturned telephone call, leaves people feeling ignored and irritated. Check your e-mail daily and send responses within a few days to those who have contacted you. Of course, you don't need to respond to unsolicited messages (also known as *spam*) unless you choose to. If you don't have time to send a full response, at least acknowledge that you received the e-mail and promise to write more soon. For example, you can e-mail her something like,

Dear Rita,

Thanks for e-mailing me your idea for a travel book. I can't wait to read it. I'll get back to you in a few days with some feedback.

Best,
Don

Ground Rule No. 2: Never E-mail a Message That You Wouldn't Want Your Mother, Your Boss, or the Rest of the World to Read

You can assume that a traditional letter *(snail mail)* is private, but it "ain't necessarily so" with e-mail. People other than the original senders can retrieve saved e-mail messages. Writing intimate or personal messages, making nasty remarks, or gossiping about an individual can lead to an embarrassing situation. Imagine how you would feel if your message showed up in someone else's mailbox or on the Internet with your e-mail address and name attached as its original sender. So don't forget, the e-mail you send and receive is never private.

Also, since many U.S. courts have ruled that companies have a right to read employees' e-mail, it is even more important to remember that your on-line messages at work are not private. If your supervisor reads your e-mails and sees an inappropriate personal message or glib remark about him or a client, you could be in an embarrassing situation.

Ground Rule No. 3: Don't Type Your Message in ALL CAPS

E-mail messages written in all capital letters are interpreted as shouting and come across as being rude. Always use upper- and lowercase letters as you would in a traditional correspondence.

Ground Rule No. 4: Keep It Short and Sweet

Studies show that people receive an average of five to ten e-mail messages a day, and many heavy users routinely have more than twenty-five messages waiting for them *each day* in their mailboxes. So, don't constantly e-mail your friends long lists of jokes, articles, or newsletters unless you know they would appreciate them. Also, to help minimize the reading time of e-mail, make an effort to keep your messages brief. However, one- or two-word responses such as "Me too," "I agree," or "Right!" can create confusion. Be sure your response includes references to the sender's original message. For example, your e-mail reply to a new friend who told you about a band playing at a local club might be:

> Hi, Eileen,
>
> Thanks for your e-mail about the band playing at Club Muzik. Rocket Science is one of my favorite groups, and I'd love to go see them this weekend. Do you want to meet for dinner before the show? I'll call you at home tonight.
>
> Bye for now,
> Don

Ground Rule No. 5: Send Well-Written Messages

Many people send their friends e-mail messages that consist of lousy typing along with an alphabet soup of abbreviations and symbols, called "emoticons" or "smilies." Informality, however, does not excuse sloppy writing, so don't send your old friends or new ones e-mail that shows a lack of attention to this important chatiquette rule. A sloppy e-mail to a client or business contact makes the sender come across as unprofessional. Take a few extra moments to proofread your messages for spelling errors (use the spell check at least twice), careless mistakes, or inappropriate comments, and put your name at the end of the message before you click on "Send." Remember, once you've sent an e-mail, you can't retrieve it.

FAQ

How do I use e-mail to make friends over the Internet?

You can make friends over the Internet the same way you do in person, via the telephone, or with a traditional "pen pal" letter. You connect and maintain contact with people who share your interests, experiences, values, and goals. In your first e-mail, always introduce yourself, explain how you got the person's name and address, and the reason for your correspondence. Like face-to-face relationships, Internet friendships need to develop naturally, over time. Your first e-mail might say something like,

> Dear . . . ,
>
> You don't know me, but my name is . . . I got your name and e-mail address from (a mutual friend, a family member, teacher, etc.). I understand that you also have an interest in . . . I live in . . . and am a college student (writer, scientist, furniture maker, etc.). I am e-mailing you to ask you . . .
>
> Sincerely,
> [Your real name and e-mail address]

Abbreviations & Emoticons

The following are just a few of the commonly used abbreviations and *emoticons,* or *smilies* (symbols), used in e-mail and on-line conversations. (Note: Abbreviations are usually in capital letters.) Also, some etiquette experts say that emoticons are fine for personal notes, but inappropriate for business-related e-mail.

Abbreviations		Emoticons	
BTW	By the way	:-)	Smile; laugh
<bg>	Big grin	:-(	Sad; too bad
<g> or <G>	Grin	:-O	Shocked

IMHO	In my humble opinion	:-D	Delighted; big grin
IOW	In other words	;-)	Wink
LOL	Laughing out loud	*	Kiss
WRT	With regard to	{{ or []	Hug

Making Conversation and Friends in Chat Rooms

Do you want to meet people and make new friends with others who share your passions and goals? It's easy if you go on-line and visit a web site with a "chat room." For example, if you like to travel, you can join an on-line discussion on driving, sailing, railroading, hitchhiking, or any other conceivable mode of transportation. Are you stumped about your next career move? Go to a business/career chat room and get some quick suggestions from other job seekers. Do you enjoy discussing current events, business trends, or your favorite

What Exactly Is a Chat Room?

A *chat room* is a web site where ongoing conversations about particular topics take place. Groups of users post e-mail messages in "real time" that everyone in the room reads simultaneously and can immediately respond to. In fact, some of the larger networks have more than 3,000 chat rooms dedicated to different topics. Chat room administrators, or *hosts,* run the discussion and clarify and enforce the rules of chatiquette. Hosts will ban users for foul language, off-color remarks, or other inappropriate behavior that violates the basic rules of communicating on-line.

recording artist's latest compact disc? There's probably a chat room where people are talking about it.

How to Find a Suitable Chat Room

Finding chat rooms is easy if you log onto services such as America Online or CompuServe, or web sites like Yahoo. com, About.com, LookSmart.com, Oxygen.com, or any number of other sites that host daily chats and "Net Events" in nearly every subject area you can think of. In their "search box," type "chat rooms" or a few words that describe your interest. (For example: "cats," "sailing," "home renovation," "movies.") In a matter of seconds you'll see lots of possible sites and chat rooms to visit. Since the names of some web sites can be misleading, it will probably take some "surfing" to find the chat rooms that are right for you.

Schmoozing On-line Requires "Chatiquette"

Good on-line conversations require many of the same skills as face-to-face conversations, including tact. You probably wouldn't ask a new acquaintance in a face-to-face conversation personal questions such as, "How much money do you make?" or "How's your sex life?" or "Is that a real diamond?" Yet something strange happens to some people who normally have good manners when they send e-mail or go into chat rooms. They throw etiquette out the window (not the computer variety) and become completely insensitive yahoos (and I don't mean the search engine!). Don't let the seemingly anonymous aspect of chatting on-line fool you. As in all conversations— whether they are in person, on the telephone, or in cyber- space—it's not just what you say; it's how you say it.

Dos and Don'ts When You Visit Chat Rooms

Most chat rooms follow normal standards of good conduct, although many on-line groups have their own sets of rules based on their audience and content. In general, the following dos and don'ts will keep you from making any major *faux pas* when you chat on-line.

Do *Lurk* Before You Leap

Lurking is observing how people in a chat room communicate before participating in the discussion. Since "chatiquette," or what is acceptable language and behavior, varies from group to group, lurking helps you decide if you feel comfortable in the chat room. Lurking also allows you to get a feel for the way messages are posted, and how to respond to questions and comments.

Don't Be Shy about Jumping into the On-line Discussion

Once you've determined that you'd like to participate in the on-line discussion, then jump in with a comment or a question, just as you would in a face-to-face conversation. The general attitude of most chat room participants is "the more the merrier."

Do Remember that You Are Talking to People

Your on-line image is based on your on-line conversation style, so let your comments reflect your sense of humor and personal interests. You can get a sense of the conversation styles of others on-line by zeroing in on the same kinds of communication characteristics you learned about in Chapter 9, "Recognizing and Using Conversation Styles."

Don't *Flame* (Insult) Other Members of the Group If You Disagree with What They Say

On-line relationships take time to develop, but only one harsh rebuke to be damaged. Just as in a face-to-face conversation, "shooting from the lip" in a chat room can cause offense. Even if you feel like e-mailing a nasty rebuke, bite your tongue (or in this case the "send" button) and don't do it.

Do Read *FAQs* (Frequently Asked Questions)

Click on "FAQ" before posting any questions to the chat room so seasoned group members don't chide you for wasting their time with already answered questions.

Don't Make Statements You Can't Back Up

Remember, just as in face-to-face conversations, trust is the basis of on-line relationships. If you make statements about yourself or others that are untrue or you cannot support, your credibility in the eyes of other on-line users will suffer.

Do Correct Your Chatiquette Goofs

When experienced users or hosts point out that you've made a chatiquette mistake, don't get upset or argue. Promptly follow their advice and thank them for calling your attention to your slip.

FAQ _____

How do face-to-face conversations differ from on-line conversations?

Some people find it easier to converse in on-line chat rooms than in a face-to-face conversation because they don't worry about appearances, and many times, the users remain anonymous. At the same time, however, without the benefits of body language and tone of voice, on-line users can miss the subtle signals that we send to one another while communicating face-to-face. (That's why emoticons were invented!) Plus, it's difficult to get to know someone well if you don't know his or her real name.

Chat Rooms Are Places to Start Conversations and Make New Friends

Chatting with people on-line is a way to broaden your circle of friends and acquaintances. There are as many places to chat and meet people as there are subjects in a bookstore. Keep in mind that the Internet is still full of *all* kinds of chat rooms, some of which are strange, on the fringe of poor taste, or downright offensive. Here, however, are a few of the more mainstream kinds of chat rooms that you can find at About. com, a real-time on-line discussion web site. Type words such as these into a search engine and you'll find many sites and chat rooms to visit:

Adoption	Crime	Health
Animals/Pets	Cultures	History
Arts/Literature	Economics	Hobbies
Business/Careers	Education	Home/Family
Chat rooms	Entertainment	Humor
Collectibles/Antiques	Environment	Internet
College Prep Courses	Games	Issues/Causes
Computers/Technology	Government	Language

Law Enforcement	Politics	Sports/Fitness
Medical	Religion	Stock Market
News/Media	Science	Talk Shows
Paranormal	Sexuality	Toys
Philosophy	Society	Travel

FAQ

I met someone in an on-line chat room whom I'd like to meet in person. Any suggestions?

It's great to move from a cyberspace conversation to a face-to-face meeting, but it requires mutual trust and common sense. If both of you are agreeable, suggest a short meeting in a public place (be specific) for a cup of coffee or snack. If you haven't exchanged photos, then say how you'll recognize each other. (For example, "I'm 5'8" tall, brown hair, and I'll be the one wearing the . . .")

Just as when you meet anyone for the first time (although you may have chatted several times on-line), *never* give out your exact address or any other personal information until you're *absolutely* sure that you want to see him or her again. Exchanging your telephone numbers could be the "next step," but only if you feel comfortable doing so.

On-line Conversations Need to Focus on People

It seems that every day new technological breakthroughs allow us to communicate with one another faster and easier. Conversing with people via e-mail and in on-line chat rooms allows you to tap into huge networks of people around the world who share your interests, dreams, or needs. People who, under normal circumstances, probably would never have the opportunity to meet, can become friends and colleagues—all simply from starting an electronic conversation.

14

Improving Your Conversations

The only thing worse than being talked about is not being talked about.
—Oscar Wilde (1854–1900),
Irish writer celebrated for his wit and flamboyance

Silence—It's Not What You Say, It's What You Don't Say

Silence has many meanings. Sometimes people fill in the blanks with wishful thinking, and assume things are meant when they aren't actually said. Silence is neither a confirmation nor a denial, and it usually leaves a question or comment unresolved.

Silence—a Negotiating Tool

Silence can be used very effectively as a negotiating device. A salesperson can present a high-powered sales pitch, speaking constantly and not giving you time to think about what is being said. Silence gives you time to think about what is being proposed. It can also encourage others to come to your side by providing them time to think about your ideas.

Silence Is Okay

Silence is natural in a conversation. Words don't have to be spoken all the time to communicate. Silence allows people to experience their immediate environment without feeling like they have to fill every void with a word. For some people, a lack of talking can be uncomfortable and can cause great anxiety. This is, for the most part, unnecessary. Silence should be considered a time to rest or think about conversation topics. If, however, silence seems more a rule than an exception, it can be a way of avoiding a particular topic or issue which you or the other person really want to discuss but are afraid to bring up.

If you sense that the other person needs some encouragement to open up, try saying something like:

You're quiet tonight. Is there something bothering you?
You seem as if something is on your mind. A penny for your thoughts.
Is there something that you want to talk to me about?

Don't push too hard if the other person doesn't respond. Instead, end your offer with something like, "If there's something that you want to say, I'm willing to listen."

Use Encouragement and Positive Feedback— Don't Criticize

Even though there is always room for improvement, when you are giving feedback it's better to praise the positive attributes of someone's efforts first, even if you really have to search for something good to comment about. It's also important not to sandwich positive comments and constructive criticism together into the same sentence. Sandwiching praise and criticism together usually turns the listener off and he becomes less cooperative and receptive to your suggestions for improvement. It's better to give praise where it is due and acknowledge the effort required to complete the task. For example, to a child who has finally finished an assignment that is way overdue: "I'm really happy to see that you've finished the assignment. It takes time to write a report that looks as good as this." Then to correct the problem of late work, you could say, "How do you think you might be able to get your next assignment in on time?" By encouraging the child with positive feedback and then presenting the problem in the form of an open-ended question, hopefully he will come up with a reasonable suggestion rather than simply do what he is told. As a result, you make it more likely that the child will respond enthusiastically to the next assignment, as well as get the work done on time.

Playful Teasing Is a Healthy Way to Convey Feelings and Attitudes

Teasing, if it is carried out in a playful and upbeat way, can be beneficial and uplifting. Teasing sensitively, not maliciously, can be an important channel of expression from one person to another. When you convey what you think and feel in a lighthearted manner, people will be more likely to consider what you are saying.

Strategy for Dealing with Put-Downs

When you are criticized with a put-down, how should you react? Keep your sense of humor up and your defenses down, and you'll be in a better position to ward off cryptic comments and let the other person know you have a confident attitude about who you are and what you do.

Don't Lose Your Sense of Humor

Bring a bit of humor into a tense or boring situation by poking a bit of fun at the people involved—especially yourself. It is important for friends to be able to laugh at themselves and at each other. We never want to lose our sense of humor, because without it, our sensitivity to criticism becomes too high. Letting people tease you a bit and laughing at yourself can be helpful when times get tough and you begin to take yourself a little too seriously.

FAQ _____

A person at work teases me with little sarcastic remarks. He's probably just making fun of me, but sometimes I think he really means what he says. What should I do?

Put-Downs Can Be a Test of Your Self-Confidence

Occasionally people put other people down to see how they react under fire. If your reactions are defensive ones, chances are good that a sensitive spot has been hit. If you laugh at yourself, and don't take the put-down too seriously, then the other person will assume you are self-confident and secure.

Ask Open-Ended Questions to Find Out the Real Reason for Put-Downs

If you feel that the other person is really serious, don't react with "Why don't you lay off," or another defensive comment.

Instead, try an open-ended question to encourage the other person to tell you what's really bothering him. This opens up the communication channels and hopefully ventilates some of the anger and frustration that causes people to put one another down. Following are some examples:

"Why do you feel that way?"

"What is it that seems to be bothering you?"

"I don't understand. What is it about ___ that is bad?"

"What is it that you don't like about ___?"

"What can I do to make you feel more positive about what I'm doing?"

The Other Person May Have Some Very Valid Things to Point Out to You

Once some of the real reasons for a person's anger come out, it's best to talk and seek a compromise solution to the problem. If a person's criticism of you is valid, try to omit responses with the words "but," "still," "however," and "yet," and substitute "Perhaps you're right! What should I have done?"

The Best Way to Get What You Want Is to Ask for It Directly

Most people prefer to be asked directly to give or do something. Many people resent demands that are not out in the open. If you want something from someone, it's better to make your request clearly. In this way, the listener knows what you are asking for, and can answer yes or no to the request, and decide to what extent, if any, she is willing to cooperate. You can't always get what you want, but at least you'll have the satisfaction of knowing you made a direct effort.

People Can't Read Your Mind

Some people expect others to know what they think, feel, and want. These people send out hidden request after hidden request, hoping that the other person will figure out what it is that they are asking for. It's better to be direct, because hidden requests are often ignored or misunderstood.

For example, consider the sulking lover who wants attention from his girlfriend. He stands gazing into a field of people at the park while his girlfriend chats with her friends nearby. He wants attention, but he doesn't want to ask for it directly, so he pouts and thinks: "I don't want to have to ask. She should know that I want her to come over here." As his girlfriend looks over and sees him alone in what appears to be a pensive mood, she thinks: "If he wanted to talk, he'd signal me to come over or walk over. It looks like he wants to be alone for a while."

In this case, the boyfriend's hidden request was not so much ignored as misinterpreted. He wanted attention, and she thought he wanted to be left alone. She can't read his mind, but that's what he expected her to do. Instead, she merely read his body language, and it seemed to say, "Stay away—I want to be left alone."

"What Do You Want from Me?"

When someone makes a hidden request, be sure that you understand what he is asking you to do. You can say, "You didn't exactly ask, but do you want me to . . . ?" This question will clarify the other person's hidden request, and then it's up to you to tell him to what extent you're willing to carry out his request. To avoid future misunderstandings that often result from hidden requests, you can say, "Please, the next time you want me to do you a favor, just ask me directly. Then I'll tell you yes or no."

50 Ways to Improve Your Conversations

Let the world know you as you are, not as you think you should be—because sooner or later, if you are posing, you will forget the pose and then where are you?

—Fanny Brice (1891–1951),
singer and comedienne

Here are some final review points to keep in mind when having conversations.

1. Be the first to say hello.
2. Introduce yourself to others.
3. Take risks. Don't anticipate rejection.
4. Display your sense of humor.
5. Be receptive to new ideas.
6. Make an extra effort to remember people's names.
7. Ask a person's name if you have forgotten it.
8. Show curiosity and interest in others.
9. Tell other people about the important events in your life.
10. Tell others about yourself, and what your likes are.
11. Show others that you are a good listener by restating their comments in another manner.
12. Communicate enthusiasm and excitement about things and life in general to those you meet.
13. Go out of your way to meet new people.

14. Accept a person's right to be an individual.
15. Show your sense of humor when talking to others.
16. Tell others what you do in a few short sentences.
17. Reintroduce yourself to someone who has forgotten your name.
18. Tell others something interesting or challenging about what you do.
19. Be aware of open and closed body language.
20. Use eye contact and smiling as your first contact with people.
21. Greet people you see regularly.
22. Seek common interests, goals, and experiences in the people you meet.
23. Make an effort to help people if you can.
24. Let others play the expert.
25. Be open to answering common ritual questions.
26. Get enthusiastic about other people's interests.
27. Balance the giving and receiving of information.
28. Be able to speak about a variety of topics and subjects.
29. Keep abreast of current events and the issues that affect all of our lives.
30. Be open to other people's opinions and feelings.
31. Express your feelings, opinions, and emotions to others.
32. Use "I" and reveal your feelings when you talk about personal things.
33. Don't use the word "you" when you mean "I."
34. Show others that you are enjoying your conversations with them.
35. Invite people to join you for dinner, social events, or other activities for companionship.
36. Keep in touch with friends and acquaintances.
37. Ask other people their opinions.

38. Look for the positive in those you meet.
39. Start and end your conversation with a person's name and a handshake or warm greeting.
40. Take time to be cordial with your neighbors and co-workers.
41. Let others know that you want to get to know them better.
42. Ask others about things they have told you in previous conversations.
43. Listen carefully for free information.
44. Be tolerant of other people's beliefs if they differ from yours.
45. Change the topic of conversation when it has run its course.
46. Always search for another person's "hot button."
47. Compliment others about what they are wearing, doing, or saying.
48. Encourage others to talk with you by sending out receptivity signals.
49. Make an effort to see and talk to people you enjoy and have fun with.
50. When you tell a story, present the main point first, and then add the supporting details afterward.

Conclusion

Here are all the tips and communication skills you need to begin and sustain conversations. Now it's up to you to get out there and meet people. You'll find that with practice, patience, and a positive attitude, you have nothing to lose and a lot to gain. Taking part in stimulating and rewarding conversations will become a reality. All you have to do is look somebody in the eye, smile, and start a conversation!

Don Gabor
Author and Communications Trainer

Don Gabor is an author, interpersonal communication skills trainer, and "small talk" expert. He helps companies that want employees with high-impact communication skills and people who want to become better conversationalists. His full-day, half-day, and hourly workshops are interactive, entertaining, and practical. In addition to customizing exercises that address the challenges of your specific group or industry, he gives each participant individualized coaching in a supportive and risk-free setting. Don uses lecture, demonstration, role-playing, hands-on exercises, and small-group activities to create an entertaining and instructional environment where everyone attending learns the meaning of personal and professional success.

Please contact Don Gabor to receive a free conversation tip sheet and more information about his books, audiotapes, videos, and workshops.

Toll-free telephone: 800-423-4203
Web site: www.dongabor.com
E-mail: don@dongabor.com

Conversation Arts Media
PO Box 715
Brooklyn, NY 11215

INDEX